THE EXPLOITATION SYSTEM OF THE
YELLOW-BILLED MAGPIE

THE EXPLOITATION SYSTEM
OF THE YELLOW-BILLED MAGPIE

BY

NICOLAAS A. M. VERBEEK

UNIVERSITY OF CALIFORNIA PRESS
BERKELEY · LOS ANGELES · LONDON
1973

UNIVERSITY OF CALIFORNIA PUBLICATIONS IN ZOOLOGY
ADVISORY EDITORS: G. A. BARTHOLOMEW, J. H. CONNELL, JOHN DAVIS, C. R. GOLDMAN,
CADET HAND, K. S. NORRIS, O. P. PEARSON, R. H. ROSENBLATT, GROVER STEPHENS

Volume 99

Approved for publication March 3, 1972
Issued February 28, 1973

UNIVERSITY OF CALIFORNIA PRESS
BERKELEY AND LOS ANGELES
CALIFORNIA

◆

UNIVERSITY OF CALIFORNIA PRESS, LTD.
LONDON, ENGLAND

591.08
C153u
v. 99
1973

ISBN: 0-520-09449-2
LIBRARY OF CONGRESS CATALOG CARD NO.: 72-619533

© 1973 BY THE REGENTS OF THE UNIVERSITY OF CALIFORNIA
PRINTED IN THE UNITED STATES OF AMERICA

CONTENTS

Introduction	1
Study Area	3
Methods	3
Environmental Timers and the Annual Cycle	5
Mating System	8
Territoriality	10
Courtship and Copulation	16
Nests	21
Eggs and Incubation	23
Nestlings	25
Fledglings	28
Life Expectancy and Fledgling Survival	30
Interspecific Interactions with Other Birds	30
Flocking	32
Roosting	35
Molt	38
Discussion	39
Summary	51
Acknowledgments	52
Appendix	53
Literature Cited	54

THE EXPLOITATION SYSTEM
OF THE YELLOW-BILLED MAGPIE

BY

NICOLAAS A. M. VERBEEK

(A contribution from the Museum of Vertebrate Zoology, University of California, Berkeley)

INTRODUCTION

THROUGH NATURAL selection each animal species has evolved a life style most suited to its environment. Whatever life style is exhibited may be assumed to optimize production of young and to maximize probability of survival of the individual and the species. The variety of life-style strategies is legion and forms the subject of a steadily growing body of comparative data, which have recently been synthesized (Crook, 1965; Eisenberg, 1966; Lack, 1968; and Tinkle et al., 1970).

In the life style of any organism time, energy, and behavior are paramount and together form a system—the exploitation system (fig. 1), earlier referred to as the "social system" (Orians, 1961). Whereas the term *social system* stresses behavior, in the *exploitation system* I wish to emphasize the importance of energy and time, which together shape the behavioral responses. *Behavior* is used here in the broad sense, including ethology and physiology.

Changes in daylength, temperature, and precipitation influence primary productivity, and this in turn results in changes in abundance and distribution of food. These aspects of energy supply in space and time affect not only seasonal and daily timing of events but also several features of a species' biology included under behavior (fig. 1). Food figures importantly in the evolution of mating systems (Verner and Wilson, 1966; Lack, 1968; Orians, 1969; von Haartman, 1969) along with the nesting dispersion (Crook, 1965; Lack, 1968), age at first breeding (Lack, 1966), size and type of territory (Pitelka et al., 1955; Tompa, 1964; Crook, 1965; Schoener, 1968), population movement (Holmes, 1966), and clutch size (Lack, 1954). Crook (1965) considers habitat and food type as selective factors in the evolution of avian social organization. I agree with him, but in the framework of the exploitation system I consider these as aspects of food. Specific types of food distribution are associated with specific habitats. Whatever type of food is selected by an organism depends on what is available and on the outcome of competition among the various species which exploit it.

In the exploitation system, time encompasses seasonal changes in daylength and climate, and daily changes in weather. The effects of daylength, temperature, and precipitation (Lofts and Murton, 1968), and food (Lack, 1954; Perrins, 1970; Ryder, 1970) on the seasonal timing and success of reproduction are well established. Daily timing of activities is influenced by weather (Verbeek, 1964) and food (Pearson, 1954; Orians, 1961) and is modified by reproduction and self-maintenance. For instance, birds feeding young spend more time per day flying than they otherwise would, and the presence of a predator may cause feeding to cease in favor of mobbing.

The behavior of an organism is thus closely responsive to and conditioned by supply of time and energy. Any changes in that supply must lead to adjustments in behavior. The exploitation system, then, is that combination of behavioral tactics which has evolved to exploit the environment to the best advantage of the species.

There are two species of *Pica*, the Black-billed Magpie (*Pica pica*) and the Yellow-billed Magpie (*Pica nuttalli*). The former is distributed widely in the Palearctic and the western Nearctic; in California it occurs on the east side of

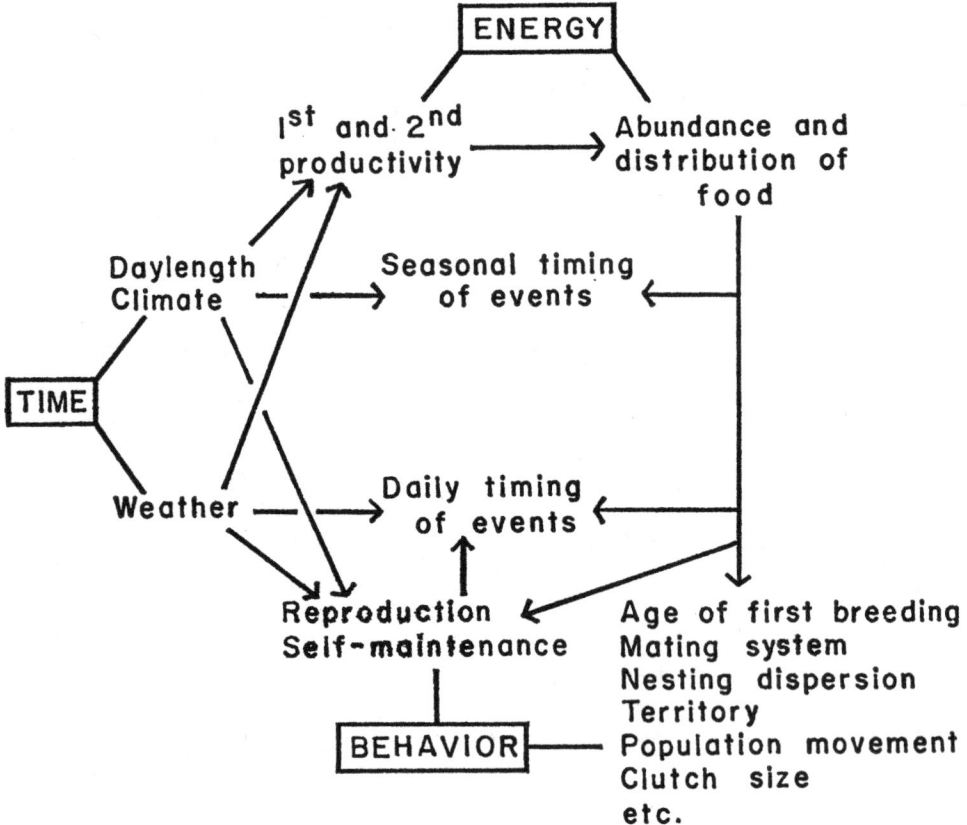

Fig. 1. Major features of the exploitation system. The arrows indicate the influence of one factor upon another.

the Sierra Nevada divide (Linsdale, 1937). This study deals with the exploitation system of the Yellow-billed Magpie, an endemic Californian species found in the annual grassland and oak savanna of the central and coastal valleys between San Francisco and Santa Barbara. I deal with the behavioral aspects of the exploitation system and show how these are related and adapted to the distribution, abundance, and availability of food, and to the seasonal changes in weather and daylength. Linsdale (1937, 1946) has reported extensively on the natural history of the species, but except for his contributions only a few short notes are available. Some aspects of the exploitation system of the Yellow-billed Magpie are compared with those of the Scrub Jay (*Aphelocoma coerulescens*) in the same area. The aspects of the exploitation system that deal more specifically with time and food supply are dealt with elsewhere (Verbeek, 1970, 1972).

STUDY AREA

Detailed studies were made on the Hastings Reservation, Monterey County, California (figs. 2 and 3) located at the upper end of the Carmel River Valley between the Santa Lucia Range and the Salinas Range. In addition I used the Blomquist ranch, bordering the Reservation on the northwest. The Hastings Reservation has been ungrazed since 1937. The Blomquist ranch is at present only moderately grazed. I used less extensively a second study area located about two miles southeast of the Reservation and straddling the divide at the upper end of the Carmel Valley. The two areas are separated and surrounded by extensive stands of chaparral, composed primarily of chamise (*Adenostoma fasciculatum*) on south-facing slopes, blue oak (*Quercus douglasii*) woodland, primarily on north- and east- facing slopes, and a mixed evergreen forest of mainly coast live oak (*Quercus agrifolia*), California white oak (*Q. lobata*) and madrone (*Arbutus menziesii*) in valley bottoms. A more detailed analysis of vegetation is provided by White (1966a). The grassland is of the California annual type (Heady, 1958) with a trend toward original, pre-grazing (partly perennial) composition on the Reservation (White, 1966b).

METHODS

This study began 15 June 1967 and ended 31 May 1971, including four breeding seasons. A total of 740 days, or parts thereof, covering all months of the year, was spent in the field.

I caught magpies and Scrub Jays with two Australian crow traps, 2 m long and wide, and 1.5 m high, baited with bread. Two birds were caught in a noose trap. Mist nets were unsuccessful. Birds were banded with U.S.F. and W.S. bands and color bands. Color bands were glued shut with acetone. Although birds in the Hastings colony are very tame, allowing approach to about 15 m, it was very difficult to trap them. Once a bird was caught, others would shy away from the trap. Adults in the Hastings colony were most readily caught in the summer, presumably because food is scarcest at that time. A history of banded breeding birds in the colony is given in the Appendix.

Adults, yearlings, and juveniles were weighed and inspected for signs of molt. A juvenile is a young of the year and it remains in this category until it completes the post-juvenile molt in October. It is then a yearling until the following October when it finishes its first complete molt. The bird is then about 18 months old. In the field juveniles and yearlings can be distinguished from adults by the brownish color of the wing tips and tail, and by the worn appearance of the latter. In proper light these characters are especially useful in the spring. In the hand birds were aged by the shape and coloration of the rudimentary 10th primary (Mayaud, 1933; Linsdale, 1937; Niethammer, 1937; Erpino, 1968a). Adults and yearlings were first sexed on the basis of weight. The maximum weight I recorded for a female was 158 g and the minimum for a male was 165 g. Once color-banded, the sex was

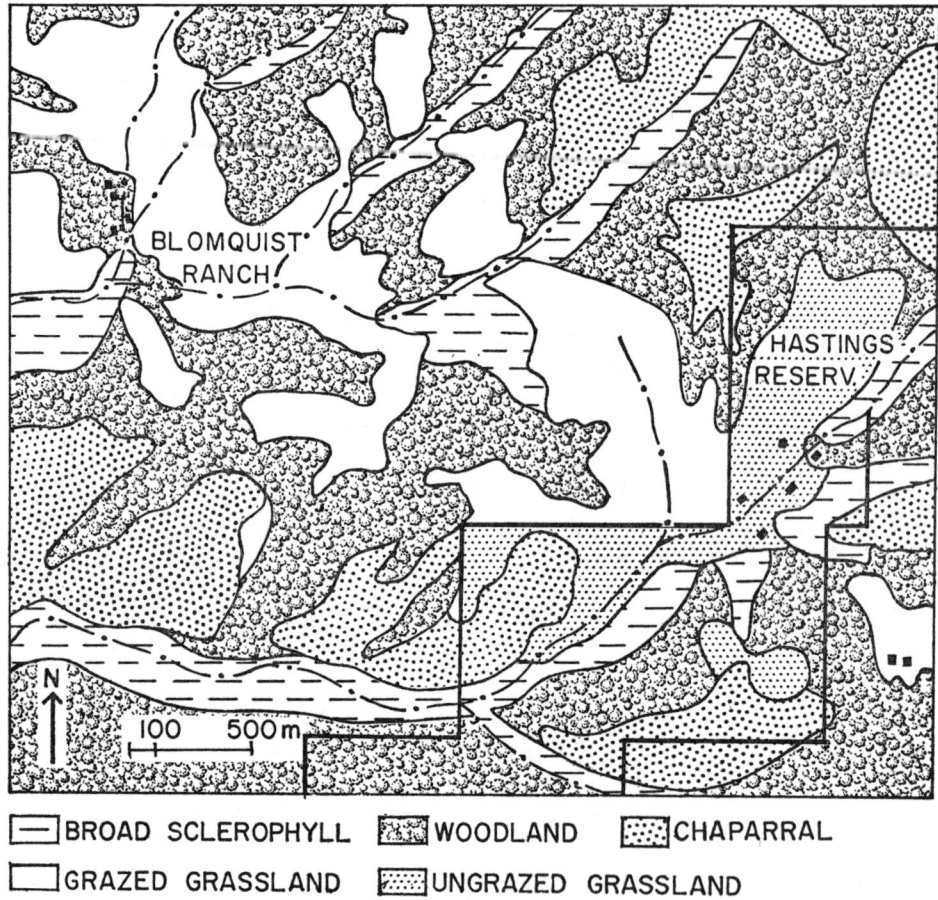

Fig. 2. Major formations of the study area.

verified in the field by behavior and size. Size should be used only when dealing with mated pairs standing near each other. Sex determination on the basis of weight proved to be correct in all cases.

Time of day is expressed as Pacific Standard Time. Weather records were obtained from a standard temperature shelter and rain gauge situated near the center of the main study colony.

As I could not readily reach nests, data pertaining to the timing of egg laying and hatching were based on behavioral clues. Copulation, the start of courtship begging (unlike other corvids, exceptionally delayed; see Courtship and Copulation), and/or the first night the female spends on the nest rather than roosting together with the male, indicate the start of egg laying. The silence of the female on the nest when the male arrives with food indicates the hatching of the eggs.

Insects were sampled in several ways, including sweep-netting, pitfall traps, cryptozoa boards, kinds and numbers detected per unit of time moving across suitable habitat, and strip censuses. These proved necessary because of the wide variety and differing ecologies of the prey eaten.

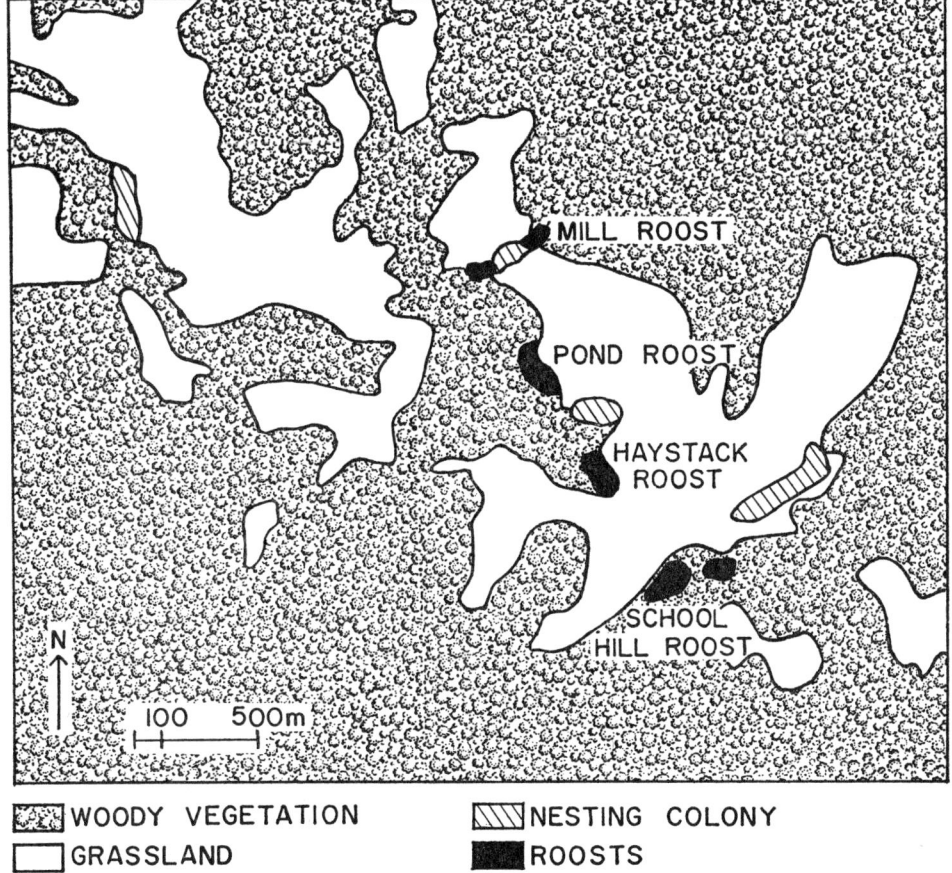

Fig. 3. Location of roosts and nesting colonies.

In 1970 data on seasonal timing of primary productivity were obtained from 10 stations, 20 yards apart. At each station the vegetation was removed from an area 400 cm square at approximately 2-week intervals. Dead and live vegetation were separated, dried at 95° C for 24 hrs, and weighed.

Territorial boundaries were established by connecting points of conflict. During the nesting phase flight distances to food sources were timed with a stopwatch. Flight speed was obtained by calculating flight time between several pairs of trees, the distance between which could be measured from an aerial photograph.

ENVIRONMENTAL TIMERS AND THE ANNUAL CYCLE

Three environmental timers—length of day and the annual cycles of temperature and precipitation—appear to be of particular importance to magpies in scheduling daily and seasonal activities.

Length of each usable day depends on time of year and on light intensity at the time magpies enter or leave the roost. On cloudy days the active day may be shortened by as much as 30 minutes. Figure 4 shows the onset and cessation of activities

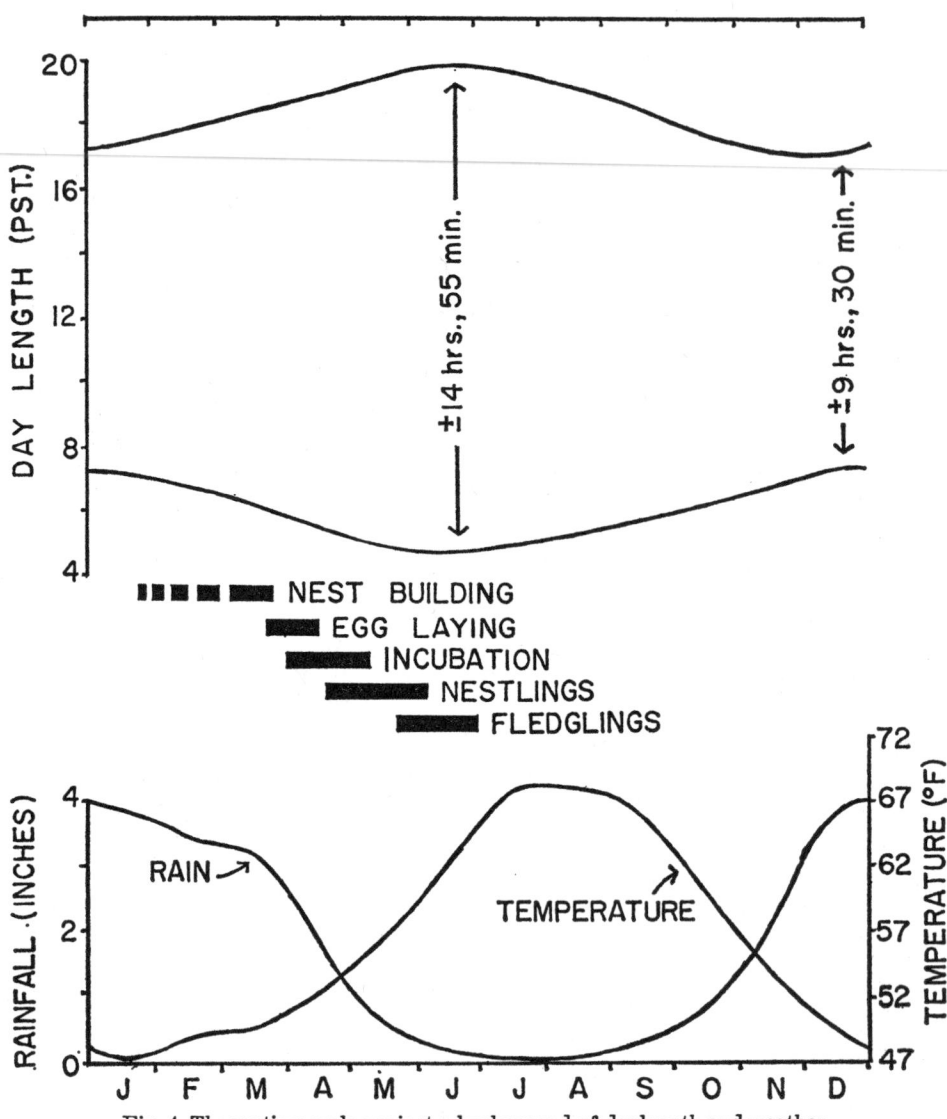

Fig. 4. The nesting cycle against a background of daylength and weather.

as determined on days with clear skies. The longest active magpie day is about 14 hours, 55 minutes, the shortest day is only 9 hours, 30 minutes.

The mean monthly temperature and total precipitation (table 1, fig. 4) are roughly inversely related. July is the hottest and driest month, January the coldest and wettest (fig. 5). The winter and spring in 1967 and 1969 were very wet, resulting in abundant, tall vegetation, while 1968, 1970, and 1971 had dry springs with relatively sparse, short vegetation.

Primary productivity of the grassland reaches its highest peak in the second half of May (fig. 6) when the greatest abundance and variety of invertebrate food is available. The reproductive effort (fig. 4) begins with nest-building in late Jan-

TABLE 1
Mean Temperatures (Degrees Fahrenheit) and Precipitation (Inches) of the Hastings Reservation

	Jan.	Feb.	Mar.	Apr.	May	June	July	Aug.	Sept.	Oct.	Nov.	Dec.
Temperature												
1967	50.0	51.0	47.9	44.7	57.1	60.6	72.4	74.4	69.0	63.0	57.2	44.9
1968	47.8	52.7	51.0	52.3	55.3	64.3	69.8	65.9	65.9	60.6	53.1	45.3
1969	47.5	43.7	48.9	50.4	57.5	59.7	69.4	72.0	68.4	57.3	57.6	49.5
1970	48.7	50.8	50.8	47.8	58.9	62.9	70.5	68.2	67.3	59.1	53.5	44.8
1971	47.6	47.9	48.1	49.4	52.7	...	...	...	...	...	...	...
1939–1968	47.0	48.6	49.3	52.4	56.0	62.0	68.4	68.0	66.4	60.9	53.7	49.2
Precipitation												
1967	5.2	0.6	5.3	7.5	0.4	0.4	0.0	0.0	0.4	0.2	1.5	2.1
1968	2.8	1.0	2.6	0.6	0.4	0.2	0.0	0.1	0.0	0.5	2.4	4.1
1969	12.1	11.6	1.6	2.4	0.2	0.2	0.0	0.0	0.1	0.3	1.1	2.2
1970	5.8	2.3	3.1	1.3	0.2	0.0	0.0	0.0	0.0	0.0	0.8	5.5	5.4
1971	1.4	0.8	1.4	2.0	0.3	...	...	...	...	...	...	...
1939–1968	3.9	3.6	3.2	2.0	0.5	0.1	0.0	0.1	0.2	0.7	2.0	3.8

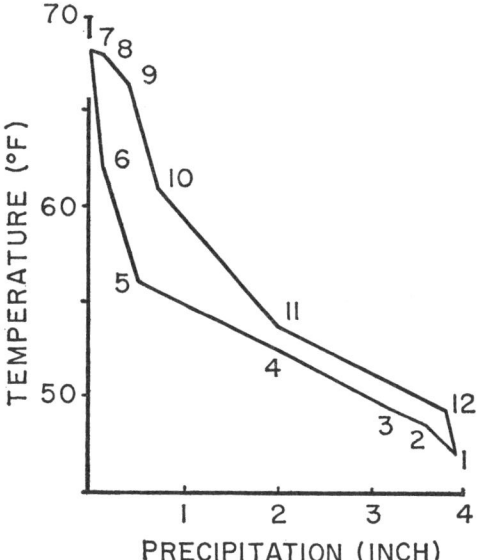

Fig. 5. Climograph of the Hastings Reservation, based on 30 years.

uary. Most of the building is done in March, and eggs are laid in early April. The eggs hatch at the end of April and early May, so that most nestlings are in the nest by mid-May, at the time of greatest food abundance. Fledging occurs in early June, and soon after that the adults and young begin to wander. The wandering phase coincides with the hottest and driest part of the year, when the vegetation dries out, the invertebrate fauna declines, and high temperatures near the ground restrict feeding to a short period after dawn and before dusk. In early September the adults show renewed interest in their home colony and former territories, and progressively more time is spent there.

MATING SYSTEM

The Yellow-bill mates for life, and members of a pair usually stay together throughout the year. They are particularly close in March during the more intensive part of the nest-building phase and in April during incubation, when the female depends almost entirely on the male for food. The relationship is more flexible during the summer wandering period, when members of a pair may separate for several hours and by distances of one or more kilometers. A pair maintains a permanent territory (see Territoriality).

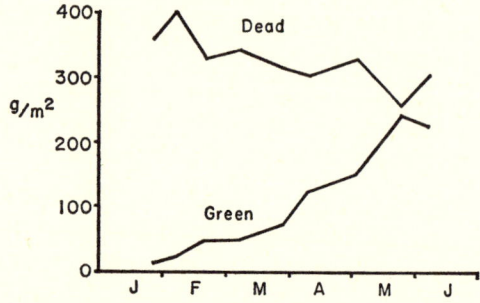

Fig. 6. Seasonal change in biomass of green and dead vegetation, based on dry weight.

Shannon (1958) compiled several instances of rapid mate replacement in the Black-billed Magpie during the nesting period. In one instance replacement occurred within seven hours. In the Yellow-bill I have found no rapid mate replacement. One female lost her mate 14 May 1969, when the nestlings were about 10 days old. She was still unmated on 1 July 1969. Similarly, a male lost his mate between 12 and 17 September 1968 and was still single on 25 September when I left the study area. On my return 20 October he again had a mate. Another male lost his mate between 20 October and 17 November and was still single on 2 January but had a mate at the end of that month. These instances indicate that mate replacement may take place at any time of the year. This information is lacking for the Black-bill.

As Yellow-bills of all ages from several neighboring colonies flock in varying degrees from about mid-June till January and February, there is ample time to find mates. Too few birds were banded to establish a hierarchy, but I have some evidence that a hierarchical system exists and that individuals recognize each other. The pair BB and RY (abbreviations of banded individuals as shown in the Appendix; see also figs. 7 and 8), for instance, evicted WG from a part of his territory in September 1968, during a time when he had no mate. Similarly, YY was in the nest tree of BB and RY several times in September 1968 and was not evicted. This bird had shown his dominance over this pair before, when he displaced them from a morsel of food. A female (RG) with fledglings, who on a previous occasion, when her mate (YY) was still alive, had chased a trespassing male from her territory single-handedly, showed reluctance to chase this same male after the loss of her mate, although she was obviously highly motivated to do so, as indicated by repeated approaches and withdrawals. Possibly her social status changed with the loss of her mate. In such a hierarchical system, and given frequent association in a flock, unmated birds of opposite sex can find each other at all times. Young of the year are mated as early as the first December of their lives, perhaps earlier. Fuchs (1957) reports similarly for the Black-bill in Germany. This may be the rule rather than the exception as suggested by Bährmann (1968), at least for *P. nuttalli*.

Several British observers (Darwin, 1874; Stewart, 1910; Brown, 1924; Selous, 1927; Shannon, 1958; Wynne-Edwards, 1962) mention noisy spring gatherings of the Black-billed Magpie in which much chasing occurs and interpret these as mating displays. Both Linsdale (1946) and Bährmann (1956) doubt this interpretation and I agree with them. In the Yellow-bill, gatherings accompanied by chasing are of two types depending on the time of the year and on which age class participates. Yearling birds often visit the breeding colony in small groups from late February to early June, but most frequently in March and April. These visits usually occur in the early morning, sometime before 08.00. The number of birds varies between two and seven. In 12 of 17 such visits an even number of birds participated, suggesting that most birds were paired. These are not mating flights, but probably a low-intensity expression of breeding activity. The birds often fly single file, stopping frequently to inspect old and new nests, from which they are chased by the adult pair on whose territory these are located. Such evictions are accompanied by much vocalizing. Brown (1924) reports similar pursuit flights in the Black-bill in England, but he does not mention the age of the participants. In five such flights that occurred from February to April the number of participants varied between four and seven, and in three instances the number was even.

Other chase-flights may be seen throughout the year, but these involve adult birds that have lost a mate and are being pursued by their neighbors. The number of birds involved is always uneven, varying from 3 to 13 birds (N = 10), depending on whether one or more pairs in the colony participate in the chase. Again, it appears that these flights are not attempts to remate but have to do with territory ownership. One male (WG) lost his mate between 12 and 17 September. Prior to the loss, the pair often fed together with a neighboring pair without any sign of enmity between them. On 17 September this neighbor male, sometimes alone, sometimes with his mate, pursued the single male several times during the day. At the time it looked as if the pair tried to evict the single male from his territory. They succeeded in this, because the following year the pair occupied the nest and most of the territory used by the lone male and his former mate the previous spring. The single male was pursued daily till 25 September when I left the study area. This male (WG) again lost his mate 2 May 1970, when his young were about 5 days old. They died shortly thereafter, presumably because they were no longer brooded. The single male was pursued by his neighbors and left his territory. Similarly, one male lost his mate between 20 October and 17 November. Other pairs in the colony chased him frequently when he trespassed. During such chases those participating call loudly and frequently, and other members of the colony show agitation.

The birds do not normally breed until 2 years old. In 1968 a pair of yearlings built a flimsy nest, a mere platform of sticks, domed with a few branches, and went as far as courtship begging but presumably laid no eggs and soon abandoned the effort. They were about one month behind the schedule of the rest of the colony. In 1970 one of two pairs of yearlings successfully bred and raised three fledglings. The springs of 1968 and 1970 were mild and probably encouraged the breeding of these yearling birds. In 1971 three pairs of yearlings built nests. One of the pairs probably had eggs in the nest but abandoned them. However, as most of the nests in the colony were abandoned on account of continued cool weather, the failure of these yearlings is no indication of their inability to raise young. Niethammer and Merzinger (1943) collected 41 Black-billed Magpies (33 ♀, 8 ♂) which were either engaged in nest-building or had eggs or young. Of the females, nine were first-year birds, as was one of the males, a total of 25 percent. In the Yellow-bill less than 10 percent of the breeding populations are yearlings. Thus, advanced one-year-olds mated to adults can participate in the breeding effort, and it appears that more females than males do so, at least in the Black-bill.

The reason why more yearling Yellow-bills do not breed is not directly apparent. There is certainly additional space within the colony and on its periphery to accommodate them, and there is no concerted effort by the adults to prevent them. Territorial behavior of adults toward those yearlings that did establish themselves in the colony was no different from that shown towards other adults. The answer must lie in limitations set by the environment. As the colony remains stable from year to year, and the adults are long-lived (theoretically the adult period lasts 8 years; see Life Expectancy), a density-dependent factor, presumably food, appears to be the reason for delayed maturation. The fact that 25 percent of breeding Black-bills in Germany are yearlings (Niethammer and Merzinger, 1943) may be due to more productive environments. My sample is far too small to test Lack's (1966) hypothesis that young birds are less efficient in raising their brood than are older birds, and therefore have fewer young.

TERRITORIALITY

Territoriality is a year-round phenomenon in the adult Yellow-billed Magpie. Although the boundaries of the breeding territory may shift from year to year, the same pair is usually to be found in its particular area of the colony (figs. 7, 8, 9, and 10). Both members of the pair defend the territory. Throughout the year males defend the territory only against males, and females against females. During the breeding season (except during the period of egg laying; see Eggs and Incubation), however, females become more aggressive and do not hesitate to drive off males as well. Visiting yearlings are more often driven off by the female than by the male, who generally merely stands by, limiting himself to vocalizations. As in the Black-bill (Erpino, 1968*b*), when I was at the nest, nestlings were more strongly defended against me by the female than by the male, who usually stayed at a distance and only approached to help in the defense when the female was present. In the defense of the territory the birds assume the tail-up posture in which the tail is held high above horizontal, the head is pointed slightly downward, and is drawn back on the shoulders. The birds walk with stiff steps and hold the wings against the body with the tips projecting above the rump. The milky white nictitating membrane is drawn over the eye, and stands out clearly against the black head. The orange spot on this membrane, reported in the Black-billed Magpie (Goodwin, 1952; Gwinner, 1966), is also present in the Yellow-bill. Although I could not see it at a distance it probably shows during the territorial display. The accompanying sound is a questioning *que* (*e* as *ea* in pear) often repeated. The more nearly perpendicular to horizontal the tail is held, the more intense the dispute. This display is best seen on the ground at a mutual territory boundary, but it also occurs in trees, on nest domes, and during the breeding season on the communal feeding ground when any two pairs come too close together. When the tail-up display occurs in a tree it is associated with vigorous bill wiping. The display is similar to aggressive wing flirting in *Pica pica* (Goodwin, 1952). One male, whom I watched over long periods, also used the tail-up display when harassed by Western Kingbird (*Tyrannus verticalis*), Scrub Jay, Brewer Blackbird (*Euphagus cyanocephalus*), and Bullock Oriole (*Icterus bullockii*).

For convenience, territoriality can be divided into three annual phases depending on expansion and contraction of the overall area and on changes in the degree of exclusiveness.

Following the breeding season from about mid-June to early September territories become smallest, and the defense is weak and largely confined to the nest tree of that spring and adjacent trees. At this time of the year the adults visit the colony infrequently for short periods and usually only one or two pairs, or even single birds, show up. At times the summer flock, containing all age classes, visits a colony. When the flock or part of it lands in a territory whose owners happen to be in the flock, these become aroused as shown by the tail-up posture and vocalizations. Probably because of the overwhelming number of trespassers, little or no chasing occurs and the display appears to have little effect.

From early September till the end of January territory size increases to include neighboring isolated trees and the ground near the center of the territory. In September the adults show an increasing interest in the territory. They frequent it more often and spend more time there, so that encounters between pairs occur more often. These encounters can take place any time of day, but they occur most frequently in the first half of the morning after the birds have fed communally elsewhere. On arrival each pair sits in the top of the tallest tree within its territory, thus becoming very conspicuous. They may remain there half an hour or more. Following such a visit to the colony all birds drift back to communal ground (Blomquist ranch) to feed together in a flock without any further hostility. This ownership display is also noted by Bährmann (1952) in the Black-bill at the onset of the breeding season. In the Yellow-bill it is a year-round phenomenon, particularly noticeable in the fall and again during the nest-building period. This display decreases in frequency and length from the end of September to December. Often neighboring pairs bicker at the common boundary of their territories early in the fall. This is when yearlings try to establish themselves, and it is their presence that causes much of the bickering, as the adults are already more or less established. By the end of November the pairs appear to have settled down, and one can predict quite accurately the number that will comprise next year's

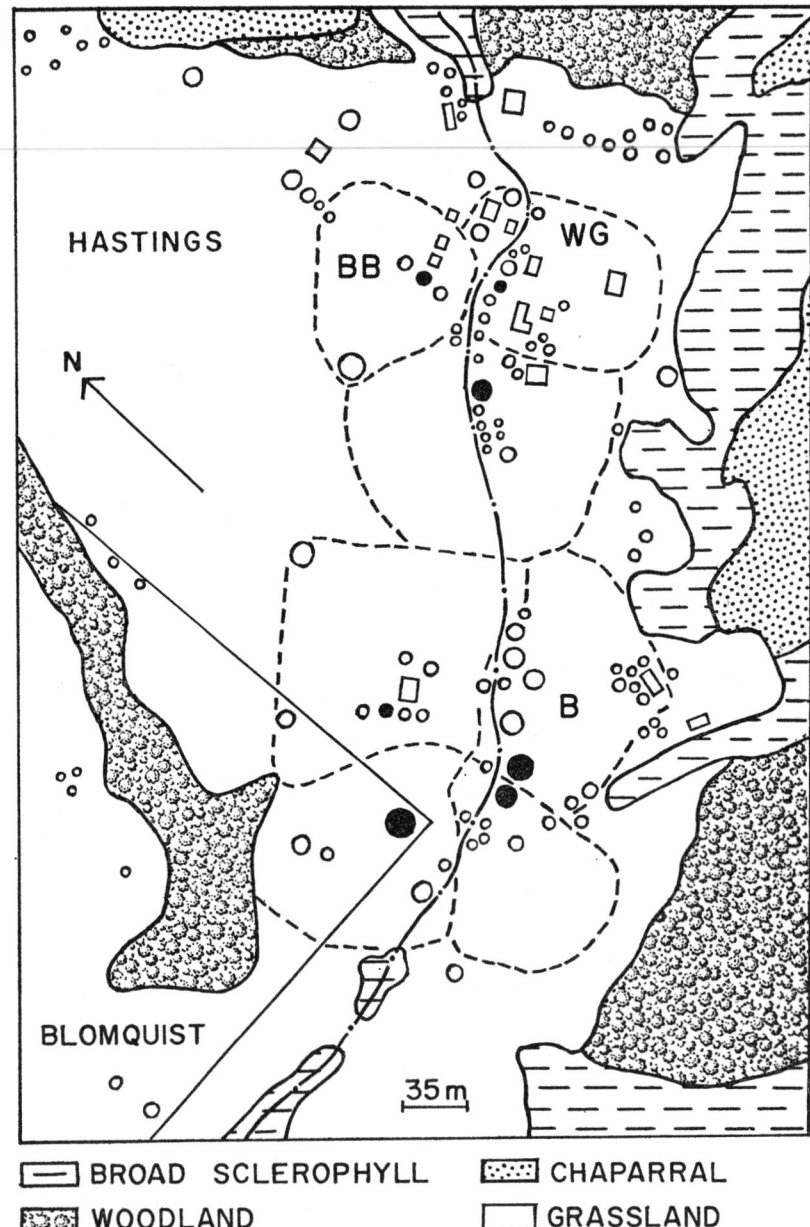

Fig. 7. The Hastings Reservation magpie colony, showing location of nests (dark circles) and approximate territorial boundaries in 1968. Letters within the territories indicate marked birds (see Appendix), open circles are trees of various sizes.

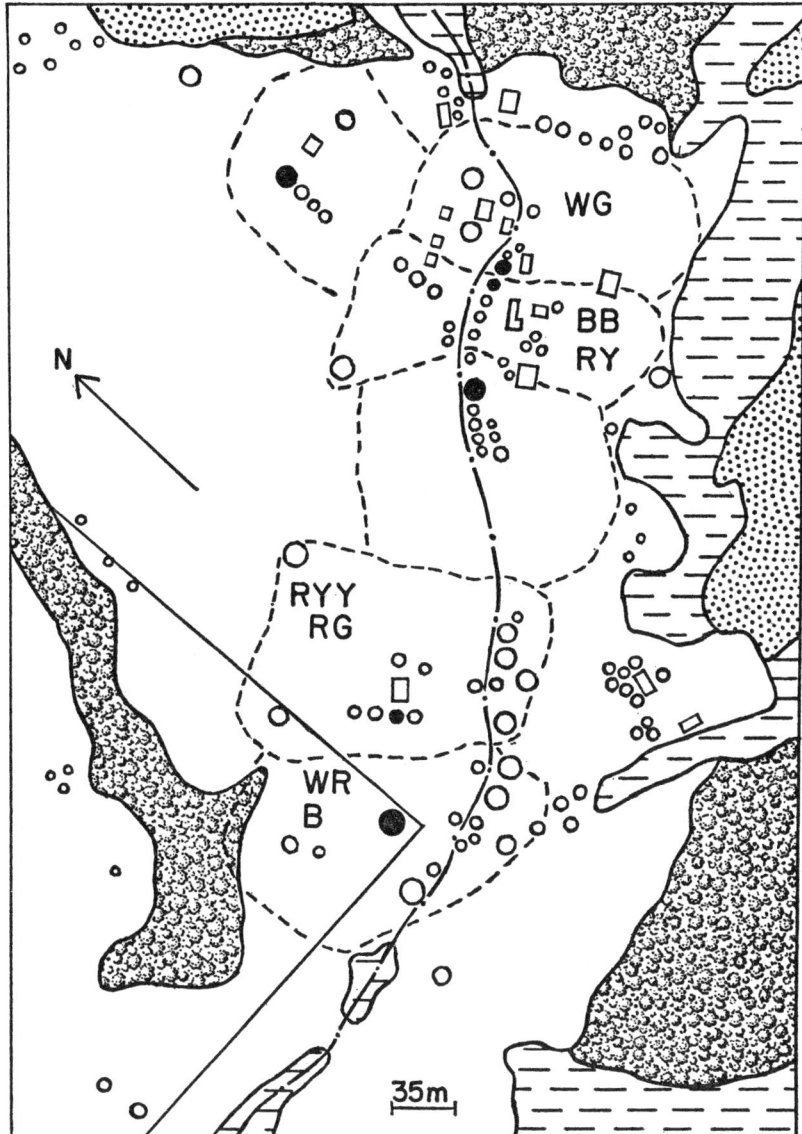

Fig. 8. The Hastings Reservation magpie colony in 1969. Legends as in figure 7.

colony. The number of adults and yearlings present in the colony from early September to the end of November varied from 7 to 16 in 1967, from 9 to 13 in 1968, and from 10 to 14 in 1969. The number of breeding pairs in the following years was 7 in 1968, 5 in 1969, and 7 in 1970. An additional adult pair appeared and entered the colony in April 1969 probably after having been disturbed elsewhere.

The earliest signs of nest-building occurred on warm days in late January. From this time on the territories expand, reaching a maximum between March and late May. Because the colony studied was drawn out along a creek, no territory was

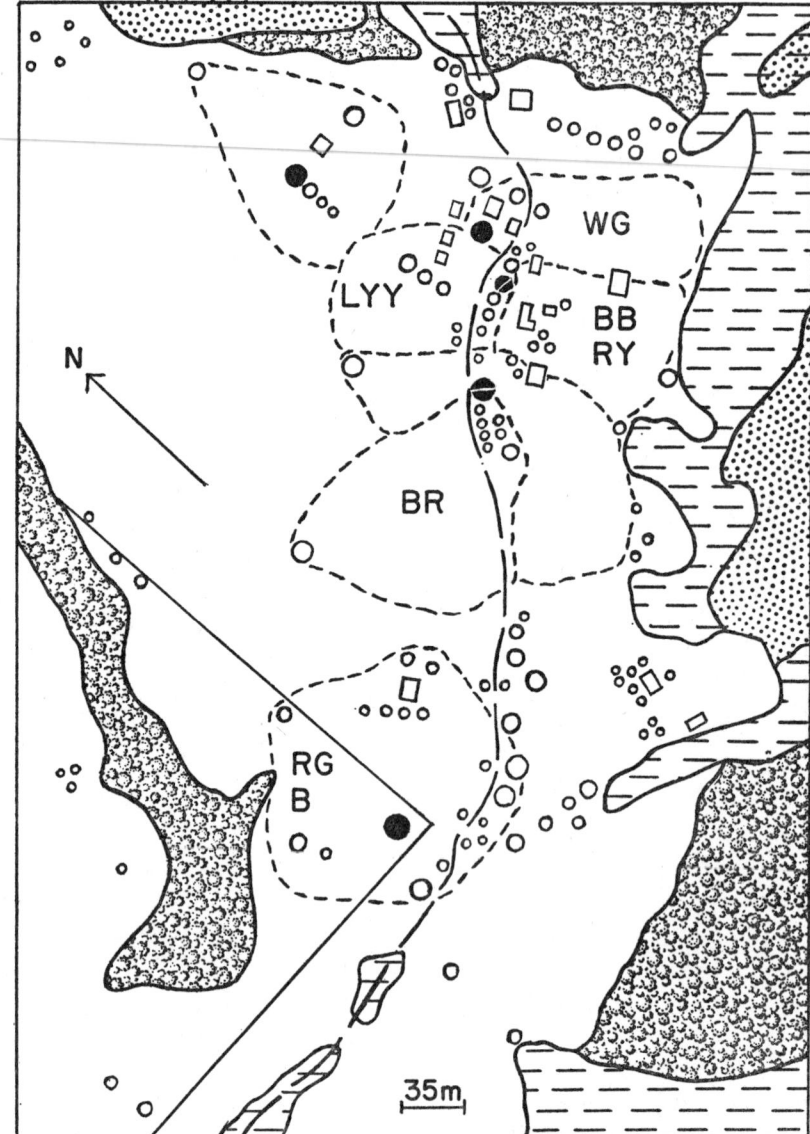

Fig. 9. The Hastings Reservation magpie colony in 1970. Legends as in figure 7.

neighbored on all sides by other pairs and all of them were thus open on the sides. This made measurement difficult. On the average the maximum territorial boundary did not go beyond 100 m from the nest. The mean size of 13 magpie territories was 1.2 ha (range 0.6–1.9 ha). The colony itself occupied about 14 ha. Although an increasing amount of the day is spent on the territory and its defense, all members of the colony continue to feed together, especially in the afternoon, at some distance from the colony. The birds mix freely with members of a neighboring colony. There is no evidence for a defended group territory as occurs in the cracticid *Gym-*

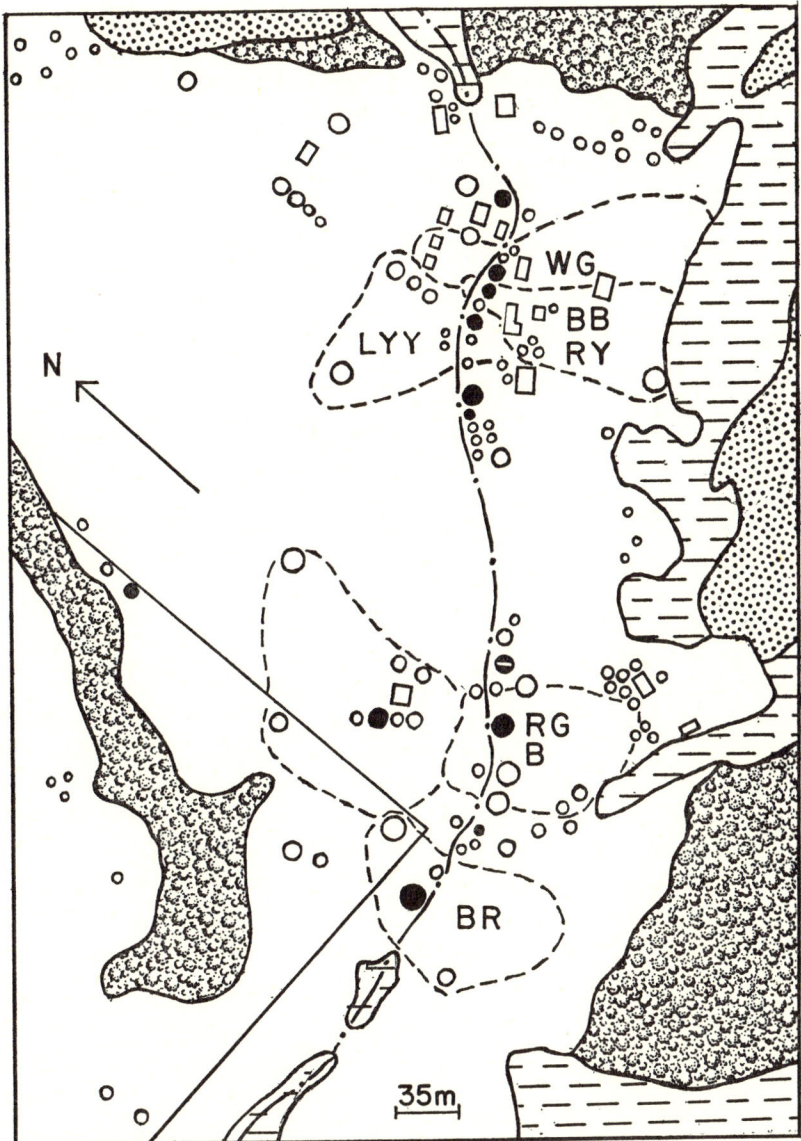

Fig. 10. The Hastings Reservation magpie colony in 1971. Legends as in figure 7. Approximate territorial boundaries were established only for six of the thirteen pairs.

norhina tibicen (Carrick, 1963). A segregation into pairs is more obvious than at other times of the year. Frequently a pair suddenly departs from the feeding group and flies to its territory. Such behavior is very contagious. At the departure of the first pair one or more others follow. Those which follow, usually neighbors of the first pair, appear to do so in great haste. On arrival on the territory each pair settles in the top of its display tree. Birds that have arrived give the tail-up display toward those flying past them en route to their own display trees. This behavior is a continuous declaration of ownership and the reinforcement thereof, and may substitute for a territorial song, which is lacking.

The degree of exclusiveness of the territory (Pitelka, 1959) changes gradually as territory size increases. During phase one and early in phase two, adults trespass on their neighbors' territory, at times even into the heart of it, and occasionally feed there. Toward the middle of phase two and throughout phase three, however, territories are exclusive. Trespassing then is limited to the periphery of the territory and almost always involves feeding birds. As a source of food the territory is most important from early March, during the peak of the nest-building, until the middle of April. During egg laying (early April) and about 10 days before that period, the pair feeds almost exclusively on its territory.

COURTSHIP AND COPULATION

I never saw the formation of a new pair in young birds or adults and hence the list of displays below may be incomplete. New pairs among yearlings are most likely formed while the birds are members of the flock. This same flock serves as a focal point to which adults that have lost a mate gravitate and where they can find new mates.

MATE PREENING

I saw this display twice and in both cases females initiated it. On 30 April, after a pair evicted a Common Crow (*Corvus brachyrhynchos*) from their territory, the two magpies flew back to their nest and the female began to nibble the lower breast feathers of her mate, who stood quietly. Similarly, on 15 September, after a territorial squabble with another pair of magpies, the territory owners flew to a tree where the female nibbled the throat and breast feathers of the male and followed this by attempts to nibble at his bill. He appeared to shun both activities. Mutual preening occurs in several species of *Corvus* (Lorenz, 1931; Skead, 1952; Lamm, 1958; Coombs, 1960; Gwinner, 1964; and Wittenberg, 1968), but apparently not in other corvids.

BILL NIBBLING

In this display members of a pair nibble and tug each other's bill. Vocalization is intermittent and of a soft warbling type. I saw this on 15 September, 25 October, 23 and 28 December, 23 March, and 15, 22, and 27 June. The example of 15 September seems to link *mate preening* with *bill nibbling*, the latter being a more advanced state of excitement. Similar behavior occurs in *Corvus* (Coward, 1920; Lorenz, 1940; Witherby et al., 1940; Skead, 1952) and also in the Tufted Jay (*Cyanocorax dickeyi*) (Crossin, 1967).

TUGGING

The male picks a leaf, a petiole, a bit of lichen, or a piece of bark and presents this to the female. She accepts it, and then the two begin to tug at it. Either one may let go temporarily and resume the tugging. At the end of the display the female always gets the object and she soon drops it. During the display both are very vocal and excited. I saw this on 3 and 24 September, 19 and 29 October, 22 December, 26 January, 18 March, 1 and 8 May, and 15, 21, and 27 June. The examples of 22 December and 18 March involved immature birds. With one exception, this display occurred on the territory. Goodwin (1952) reports similar behavior in the European Jay (*Garrulus glandarius*).

The three kinds of display apparently occur throughout the year and probably aid in maintaining the pair bond. These displays also form antecedents to courtship feeding and are to be seen as a graded series of increasing sexual commitment. The example of 15 June appears to provide the evidence:

"At 17.55 some adults come to the colony after several hours of absence. BB and RY evict a pair of strangers who come too close to the nest. After the eviction, they begin to nibble each other's bill. Then RY picks a leaf and they tug on it till it breaks. She quivers her wings as in low intensity courtship feeding display. They are interrupted by the return of the two trespassers and when these depart the pair again begins to nibble each other's bill, followed by tugging at a leaf and a piece of bark. Then he presents her pieces of bark, each of which she accepts and then discards. At 18.10 they fly away and join some others to feed."

COURTSHIP BEGGING AND FEEDING

The begging call of the female, an often repeated *quay?*, signals the beginning of egg laying. She calls throughout the day and at times hops to the male and crouches in front of him with fluttering, partly opened wings held away from the body and the underside turned forward; the tail is kept closed and held down at its usual angle, and the partly opened bill points upward at about 40°. When crouched in front of the male, the female utters the begging call more rapidly than when she is off by herself. Both posture and call are apparently the same as those used by fledglings begging food from their parents.

In one established pair that I watched closely, the female began to beg on 6 April. She laid the first egg on 8 April. Her calls were hoarse and produced infrequently during the day. The next day the sound had lost its hoarse quality and the calls were delivered more frequently, reaching the largest number per hour on the fourth day (table 2). In the first few days the male appeared reluctant to feed his begging female and often avoided her overtures by hopping away when she crouched in front of him. His rate of feeding her gradually increased, but it was still relatively low on the fourth day in spite of the barrage of calls from his mate (table 2). Between the fourth and sixth day the number of begging calls dropped drastically but the feeding rate continued to rise. At that time the female was incubating about 60 percent of the day (table 3). The curves of courtship begging and feeding, then, are out of phase, with the former reaching its peak earlier. Apparently the female needs to begin begging early and at a frequent rate to stimulate the male to feed her. Once this is achieved she slackens, while his feeding continues at about the same pace through incubation, during which time she depends on him for almost all food.

When feeding the female, the male stands in front of her and feeds her without any special display on his part. Often his neck and head are pushed back and sometimes he has to take a few steps backward because of the excitement and apparent eagerness of the female. He usually feeds her quickly and then moves away. During feeding the female's begging call changes to a feeding call, a throaty

TABLE 2
Courtship Begging and Feeding Rates of One Pair

	Total minutes observed	No. times ♂ feeds ♀	Feeding rate per hour	No. begging calls	No. begging calls/hour
Pre-egg laying					
7 April[1]............	194	0	0	1957	605
Egg laying					
8 April[2]............	450	1	0.13	5344	713
9 April.............	140	3	1.29	1770	759
11 April............	608	26	2.57	2928	289
12 April............	180	14	4.67	792	264
Incubation					
15 April............	350	16	2.74	345	59
16 April............	450	22	2.94	538	72
22 April............	300	14	2.80	369	74
23 April............	415	23	3.33	596	86
25 April............	93	6	3.87	153	99
29 April............	403	18	2.68	362	54
30 April............	415	16	2.31	304	44

[1] Courtship begging began 6 April but number of calls not recorded.
[2] First egg laid on 8 April as determined from behavioral observations.

quay-quay-qeck-qeck-eck-ock-ock-ow-ow-ow. Each of these syllables is included in the total counts of table 2. On the average the feeding call has 23 syllables. The feeding call is used almost exclusively once incubation has started.

In one pair of Scrub Jays I saw courtship feeding six days before the first egg was laid. The male continues to feed the female throughout incubation. The female does not beg for food as does the Yellow-bill. While being fed the female jay assumes the same posture and movements as the Yellow-bill. I heard no vocalization, perhaps because I was too far away. The occurrence of courtship feeding among other corvids is summarized by Skutch (1960).

COPULATION

The first attempt at copulation in one closely watched pair occurred on 3 April 1969. The pair was feeding in a meadow when the female found a morsel of food which she held in her bill. The sight of this apparently excited the male who approached her with flapping, partly opened wings. The birds were silent. Standing beside the female, the male lifted one leg and extended it to the female's back. At the same time he kept the other leg and his body as far away from her as possible. She ate the morsel and walked away. I noticed the same behavior the previous spring, except that the female held some pieces of grass in her bill instead. Courtship begging had not yet begun in these two females, and the display was of low intensity.

I saw successful copulation twice, both times on the ground. On 28 March 1970 a female pecked at her leg band, and apparently this incited the male to begin his pre-copulatory display, as described below. The next day while the female was

TABLE 3

NEST ATTENTIVENESS DURING EGG LAYING AND INCUBATION
(based on one nest)

Date	No. of sessions	Total minutes	Female on nest	Percent attentive
8 April[1]	2	405	156	38.6
9 April	1	120	36	30.0
11 April	2	608	367	60.4
12 April	1	180	150	83.1
15 April	3	350	330	94.4
16 April	3	450	405	90.1
22 April	2	300	273	91.1
23 April	3	415	397	95.7
29 April	3	403	368	91.4
30 April	3	416	382	91.9

[1] First egg laid. Clutch completed on 13 April.

feeding, the male approached her flapping his wings and calling *wock, wock* softly, and he mounted her. While the male stood before her the female moved her wings as if she were begging. Her first begging calls did not occur until 31 March. These data agree with those for *Pica pica* (Bährmann, 1968).

Frequently copulation attempts follow courtship feeding, but I have never seen these to be successful. After the male feeds his mate, she usually continues to beg as if she expects more. If she persists, the male may become sexually motivated and begin his display. He tries to sidle up to her with flapping, fully opened wings held at about a 50° angle to the ground with the underside facing forward. He keeps his body erect. The female keeps moving away and he follows her awkwardly, giving phrases from his "courtship song." In its full form it sounds like *wock, wock, wock-a-wack, wock, pjur, weer, weer,* which is then repeated. The last three syllables are high in pitch, drawn out, and sound rather delicate for a bird this size. Prior to copulation the *wock* part is most often used, and it is rendered faster than when the bird just gives the song.

As at least some copulations occur before courtship begging begins, the two activities are apparently not related. The probable ultimate significance of courtship begging in the Yellow-billed Magpie is that it prepares the male to feed the female during incubation. This seems clear in that begging begins at a time when the female still finds all or most of the food for herself (table 2). It is not the food given her then, but his continued feeding of her later, during incubation, which is important. The importance of courtship begging to maintenance of the pair bond would appear to be secondary at this time. Five times I saw females begging food from their mates after their young had fledged and thus well past the time when they depended on the males for food. The significance of begging at this time is not clear, but as at least two of these instances were associated with territorial conflicts, it may serve to reinforce the pair bond.

During the courtship-begging period the females appear to be oblivious to their surroundings. While on the ground the females appear to be feeding, but actually they often seem just to walk without purpose. Twice I saw females hop to a strange male and beg food from him. Before the courtship-begging period they would not have tolerated such males on their territories. Associated with this is the fact that during this period one sees males in places away from their own territories. They come in response to the begging calls of the females and sit near them on the periphery of the foreign territory, calling *wock, wock* at a slow rate of about 30 per minute.

On 8 April a female begged in front of a strange male at the periphery of her territory. Her mate noticed it, came flying towards them, and chased the strange male away. The rightful male then chased his female back to the nest area, pursuing her closely. On 10 April the same strange male again approached the same female. As he landed near her, she hopped toward him and begged from him. He flew away about 15 m and appeared cautious. She followed as he flew to a fence post. Then she flew to the ground and he, still looking around cautiously, followed her and jumped on her back. At this point the rightful male came flying to them and the foreign male departed. The female was chased back to the nest as before. On 13 April a mated pair copulated in the grass about 20 m from the nest tree. When they were barely finished a foreign male appeared, and while the rightful male flew off the female and to his own nest tree, the foreign male tried to copulate forcefully. She escaped and he fled when the rightful male returned. On 28 March a female begged from her mate. She then flew to the ground near to where a yearling was feeding. The male followed the female and when he approached the yearling, it apparently flicked its wings in appeasement. The male took it as an invitation to copulation and began to court. Every time he tried to mount the yearling it jumped away. After about 40 seconds the male gave up, ruffled his feathers, and began to feed. During all this time the female was about 1 m away and continued to beg. Five of the six males in the colony in 1969 were seen to attempt copulation with foreign females on eight occasions. Of these, seven were attempts at copulation in response to the begging call of the female and only one was a case of interference in response to the visual stimulus of a copulating pair. None of the copulations witnessed appeared successful, but the possibility that some are carried to completion cannot be excluded.

In the Rook (Coombs, 1960) incubating females are frequently raped by strange males. The same occurs in the Carrion Crow (Wittenberg, 1968) and there is one record for the Raven (Kramer, 1932). As incubation is already in progress such attempts at rape have no genetic consequence, in contrast to the Yellow-billed Magpie, where rape does occur during the egg-laying period. Coombs suggests that the incubation posture of the females is very similar to the female pre-copulatory posture and thus invites rape on the nest. Because of the domed nest the female magpie is concealed from view, and copulation there is made difficult if not impossible. There is good correlation between degree of coloniality and rape, attempted rape, and interference. To put it another way, the smaller the territory (Rook), the greater the chance of rape. The Yellow-bill lies between the Rook and the Carrion Crow; and the Raven is last in this sequence, having the largest territories.

In addition to clear visibility and proximity of the sexes in a colony, the continuous loud begging of the female is probably a strong stimulant to all males in the colony. Males whose females are not yet receptive or are no longer receptive may be drawn to other females who loudly proclaim their receptivity. This is apparently what happens as shown in the following two examples. On 8 and 10 April, one male, whose female did not lay her first egg until 19 April, attempted to rape a female who laid her first egg on 8 April. Similarly, on 8 April, a male, whose own female had started to lay on 26 March, attempted to rape a female who laid her first egg on 7 April.

NESTS

Magpie nests are large domed structures which may survive for a number of years. Often the dome caves in before the nest is a year old, but in some nests it remains in place for several years. In the summer of 1967 I counted 36 nests of various ages in the colony. With the addition of 6 new nests in 1968, 5 in 1969, and 6 in 1970 there were 37 nests in the summer of 1970. Thus, on the average, a nest was recognizable as such for about 6 years after it was built.

Yellow-bills show a year-round interest in their nests. Prior to the wandering phase, the fledglings visit most of the nests in their parents' territory. During the wandering phase, whenever they visit the home colony or another one, the juveniles inspect nests, walk on them, or go inside if possible. They do this throughout their first year and particularly in their first spring, when apparently they are weakly motivated to breed. The adults show a similar interest, but theirs is more restricted to their own nest of the year or to an intact nest of a previous year. At times they visit nests of other adults, and this leads to territorial squabbles. The adults show particular interest in their nest of the year in September–October following the wandering phase. This may be because it is also the time when the yearlings explore the colony for a possible vacant territory, in the process of which frequent clashes occur on or around nests.

Typically the birds build a new nest every year. False nest-building as reported for the Black-bill (Huber, 1944) did not occur. Only four times were old nests used and this involved the same pair of birds each year. The mean distance between 12 nests of separate neighboring pairs, located in territories connected by a continuous canopy of riparian woods, was 31 m (range 7–44 m). In three instances two pairs nested in the same tree at distances of 7 m, 12 m, and 12 m. One of the trees also contained a Scrub Jay nest. The nests are usually placed high off the ground and at the periphery of the canopy. The average estimated height of 29 nests was 16.9 m (range 9–24 m) and 50 percent of them were above 16 m. For comparison, about 50 percent of 128 Black-billed Magpie nests were above 3.2 m, and only 17 of the 128 were above 6.3 m (Erpino, 1968b). In Denmark the average height of 300 nests was 4 m (range 1–12 m); 50 percent were at 3 m or lower, and about 84 percent at 4 m or lower (Hansen, 1950). This fundamental difference between the two species is also reported by Linsdale (1937). The difference in nest height is probably related to predation (Crook, 1965).

Four times in the fall I saw magpies placing a stick on nests used that spring or a previous year. In all cases the sticks were obtained from the pair's old nest and then redeposited, or from another nearby old nest. This apparent resurgence of nest-building is probably a by-product of courtship activity, because on two occasions it followed the leaf-tugging display. In each case only one stick was just dumped on the nest and then abandoned. None of the nests was used the next spring. Some pairs in the colony begin to build in late January, and some evidence suggests that birds building for the first time tend to start later than older ones. By mid-February all birds are building. Early in the season building is confined to sunny days, but in March, at the peak of building, the birds also work when the sky is overcast; however, more sticks are added on sunny days. Bouts of building, from 1 minute to as long as 52 minutes, are interrupted by bouts of feeding, preening, and chasing trespassing yearling magpies. Most building occurs in the morning as is true for the Black-bill (Labitte, 1953). The nest is finished by the end of March.

TABLE 4
SOURCE OF NEST MATERIAL AND ROLES OF THE SEXES
(based on one nest)

| Date | Period | Sticks obtained from |||||| Mud, grass || Total ||
| | | Ground || Tree || Old nest || | | | |
		♂	♀	♂	♀	♂	♀	♂	♀	♂	♀
14–15 March[1]	08:00–13:00	8	1	14	23	4	5	6	0	32	29
16 March	07:30–13:00	15	4	23	14	3	12	11	9	52	39
23–25 March[1]	06:00–13:00	14	3	6	19	2	1	16	10	38	33
Total		37	8	43	56	9	18	33	19	122	101
Percent		26		58		16				54	46

[1]Combining all minutes of consecutive days, which together represent a whole day (Verbeek, 1972).

Both sexes participate in the nest-building (table 4). In the second half of March, during 17.5 hours of watching at one nest, the pair brought 171 sticks to the nest. Most of these (58 percent) were obtained by breaking them from dead branches in the nest tree and other trees in the territory. Second in importance were sticks found on the ground (26 percent). Sticks obtained from old nests (16 percent) were pulled primarily out of the domes. Only once did a bird steal a stick from a new nest; the owners were absent. Part of the apparent suspicion among adult pairs during the nest-building season may stem from such thievery. There appears to be a division of labor, with the larger male concentrating on nest material obtained from the ground, and the smaller female on material from the tree and old nests (table 4). The female does most of the inside of the nest, especially the shaping of the nest bowl. Most of the mud used for the outer nest-lining is brought by the male who gives it to the female. In the very dry spring of 1971 cow dung was used instead of mud. The use of mud in nest construction may be a limiting factor in magpie distribution in dry areas. On the other hand, the ability to use cow dung may have helped the species to penetrate some arid areas, where man has introduced cattle.

One nest that I dismantled contained 1,573 sticks. Of these, 1,250 were in the dome and 323 in the bowl. The total weight was 10,585 g. To this must be added the weight of the nest-lining, mud, cow dung, and bits of sticks fastened in the mud, giving a total of 11,270 g. This is about 70 times the weight of an adult magpie.

EGGS AND INCUBATION

Following completion of the nest the pair primarily feed and loaf for about 10 days. Early in this period the female visits the nest a few times to add some nest-lining. The pair remain more or less on the territory, but periodically, especially in the afternoons, several pairs may feed communally, although rigidly in pairs, at a short distance from the colony. Erpino (1968b) reports for the Black-billed Magpie a similar period of relative inactivity between completion of the nest and the laying of the first egg. Building the nest is a very strenuous task. The sticks, often longer than the birds themselves, frequently become entangled in the branches of the nest tree, and the birds often have to make several stops on their way to the nest. The 10-day period is probably needed to recuperate and to build up surplus energy in the female for egg production. Following this period the eggs are laid daily between 06.30 and 08.00. In England Brown (1924) finds daily laying in the Black-bill, but Holyoak (1967), reporting on data collected on nest record cards, finds that about 20 percent of the eggs are laid at intervals of 2–3 days. Bährmann (1968) reports daily laying in Germany. Black-bills in North America lay one egg per day (Erpino, 1969) or generally one per day (Jones, 1960).

Toward the end of the 10-day period the female begins her courtship begging. One closely watched female began to beg on 6 April and laid her first egg on 8 April. Initiation of egg laying in the colony appears synchronized, but not any more so than in the non-colonial Scrub Jay. In 1969 the estimated extreme dates for clutch initiation were 29 March and 9 April in six magpie nests, and 1 and 9 April in five Scrub Jay nests. Social stimulation among the magpies in the colony does not seem to play a role in the start of egg laying. Instead, the similarity of the egg-laying period of the Yellow-bill and the Scrub Jay appears to depend on an environmental timer.

Incubation begins before the clutch is completed (table 3). This is also apparent from the asynchronous hatching of the eggs. In one nest of six nestlings, of which the oldest was about 6 days old, two of the young were only two-thirds as heavy as the others, and in a nest of five nestlings (3 days old) one young had only half the weight of its siblings. In the Black-bill incubation begins after several eggs have been laid, but sometimes it starts with the first or last egg (Holyoak, 1967). Erpino (1968b) also mentions variability in this respect.

Among corvids, the genera *Pica* and *Cyanopica* (Hosono, 1966) have the largest clutches. Because of the inaccessibility of the nests I can offer no new data on clutch size. One nest visited about three days after the eggs hatched had five nestlings and one unhatched egg that was removed by the parents after three more days. This was probably a clutch of six eggs. Another nest had six nestlings. Linsdale (1946) reports 6.5 eggs as the average of 70 Yellow-bill clutches. O'Halloran (1961) reports a mean clutch size of 6.48 based on 684 completed clutches of the Black-billed Magpie in Montana, and Erpino (1968b) finds means of 6.5 (29 nests) and 6.1 (31 nests) in Wyoming. In England the mean clutch size of 179 sets is 5.6 (Holyoak, 1967). From data collected by Labitte (1953) in France between 1908 and 1952 I calculate a clutch size of 6.4 eggs. Huber (1944) reports clutches of nine and ten eggs in Germany and states that these were collected in years when May beetles were plentiful. The mean weight of eight eggs in a single clutch of the Yellow-bill was 8.3 g (range 7.5–8.8 g) (Linsdale, 1937).

Only the females incubate. Prior to egg laying and incubation the females spend no time sitting on the empty nest as reported for the Brown Jay (Skutch, 1960), Blue Jay (Hardy, 1961), and Tufted Jay and Mexican Jay (Crossin, 1967). As soon as the first egg is laid the females spend part of the day on the nest. In one closely watched nest this amounted to 38.6 percent. During this time the female still sought her own food, and the periods on the nest were short and interrupted by bouts of feeding. Toward the end of the laying period time spent on the nest increased to 83.1 percent. Following the egg-laying period she was on the nest an average of 92.3 percent of the day, and her attentiveness remained stable throughout the period (table 3). Erpino (1968b) reports nest attentiveness during incubation of 84 percent in the Black-bill.

TABLE 5
FEEDING RATE OF THE FEMALE BY THE MALE DURING INCUBATION[1]

Period	Total hours 1968	Total hours 1969	No. of feedings 1968	No. of feedings 1969	Feedings per hour 1968	Feedings per hour 1969	Attentiveness (1969) Total minutes	Attentiveness (1969) Percent attentive
07:00–10:00	17	11	58.0	34.0	3.4	3.1	540	94.9
10:00–13:00	4	16	11.5	50.0	2.9	3.1	540	93.4
13:00–16:00	12	10	19.5	29.0	1.6	2.9	540	95.2
16:00–19:00	9	9	16.0	15.0	1.8	1.7	520	87.5
Total	42	46	105.0	128.0				
Mean					2.5	2.8		

[1]These observations are based on several nests, except for attentiveness, which is based on only one nest.

The high percentage of attentiveness is made possible because the male feeds the female on the nest. His rate of feeding her increases rapidly in the egg-laying period, but from the time the last egg is laid until the end of incubation it remains rather stable at about three feedings per hour (table 2). When the data are analyzed on a daily basis, the feeding rate per 3-hour period (table 5) drops only slightly between 07.00 and 16.00, but is considerably less in the three hours before nightfall. The percentage of inattentiveness of the female follows this trend, showing stability for most of the day but increasing toward nightfall (table 5). Apparently the male is not able to obtain enough food for himself and his mate to last them through the night, which is about 10.5 hours during the period of incubation. Of 113 feedings seen during the incubation period, 88 (78 percent) occurred while the female was on the nest, 17 (15 percent) while she was off the nest but in the nest tree, and 8 (7 percent) while she was away from the nest tree. The periods of inattentiveness of the female are largely determined by the feeding schedule of the male. If he stays away too long, the female may come off the nest when she sees him coming. At times the female leaves the nest to feed or defecate. Defecation always occurs away from the nest, but within the territory.

Her feces were very thin and watery and rather strikingly yellow in appearance. The average of 23 inattentive periods was 4.1 minutes (range 1–7.5 min).

NESTLINGS

When the eggs hatch, the female no longer utters the feeding call when the male comes to the nest with food. The colony becomes very silent. The female alone broods the young, and she does so in decreasing amounts of time for about the first 15–16 days (table 6). During this period she leaves the nest increasingly more often to find food for herself and the young. In the early stages of brooding the male alone feeds the young and probably also feeds the female. At first her feeding rate (table 7) is below that of the male, but once the brooding period is past the rates are about equal. A progressive decline in feeding rate occurs in both sexes, which correlates with a gradual increase in the flight distance to the food source, particularly noticeable in the female (table 7, last column). As nearby

TABLE 6
PERCENT ATTENTIVENESS OF FEMALES BROODING NESTLINGS
(data from two nests)

Nest	Date	No. of sessions	Total minutes	Female on nest	Percent attentive
12........	8 May[1]	2	360	170	47.2
	9 May	3	395	160	40.5
	10 May	1	90	38	42.8
23........	1 May[2]	2	233	176	75.5
	2 May	3	300	221	70.4
	3 May	3	300	177	59.0
	8 May	4	467	150	32.1
	9 May	2	180	19	10.6
	10 May	2	120	25	20.8

[1]Nestlings about 8 days old.
[2]Nestlings about 5 days old.

food sources become exhausted the birds have to fly farther to exploit new ones. This is also evident in the types of food the nestlings receive. Besides food obtained from the individual territories, the colony used three major areas farther away. The first and nearest site, about 250 m from the center of the colony, produced mainly Tipulidae. It was used in 1968 and 1969, when tipulids (Diptera) were abundant. The birds continued to use it, but in addition they began to exploit a second feeding area, about 450 m from the colony center. The characteristic food item here was *Ceuthophilus californianus* (Orthoptera). This site was not used extensively in 1968, 1970, and 1971. Toward the end of the nestling period most food, primarily pupae of *Malacosoma constrictum* (Lepidoptera), came from an area about 950 m from the colony center in 1968, 750 m in 1969, 750 m in 1970, and 800 m in 1971.

With so much food obtained at long distances from the nest, of what importance is the territory as a food source? Of the number of feedings listed in tables 2 and 5, I also recorded whether the food was obtained on or off the territory. For instance, of the 16 feedings on 16 April (table 2) 10 were obtained on the territory,

TABLE 7
Feeding Rate and Distance to Food Source During Nestling Period
(data from one pair of birds)

	Total minutes	No. of feedings	Feedings per hour	Total time to and from food source (seconds)	Mean distance to food source (m)[1]	Mean distance of consecutive days[2] (m)
Male						
8 May[3]	360	25	4.2	2264	528	
9 May	395	30	4.6	2131	414	463
10 May	90	7	4.7	525	438	
16 May	414	32	4.6	3012	549	
17 May	321	19	3.6	1326	407	498
18 May	90	3	2.0	274	533	
25 May	347	19	3.3	1290	396	
26 May	420	19	2.7	2084	640	518
Female						
8 May[3]	360	13	2.2	998	448	
9 May	395	18	2.7	1149	372	408
10 May	90	5	3.3	370	432	
16 May	414	23	3.3	2687	649	
17 May	401	23	3.4	1834	465	610
18 May	90	6	4.0	923	898	
25 May	457	21	2.8	2287	635	
26 May	420	19	2.7	2847	874	749

[1] Average rate of flight is 0.7 km per minute.
[2] Total minutes of consecutive days represent all minutes of total day (Verbeek, 1972).
[3] On 8 May the nestlings were about 8 days old.

6 off it. By plotting the off-territory feedings as a percentage of all feedings for each day, figure 11 was obtained. At the beginning of incubation the male collected most of the food for himself and his mate from the territory, but as incubation progressed proportionately more food came from off the territory. During the first week of the nestling period both parents obtained most of the food off the territory. At the end of this period (12 May) the male disappeared, and the remainder of figure 11 is based on a neighboring pair whose nestlings were as old as those of the first family. The females of both nests continued to obtain food almost exclusively off the territory, but the male progressively reverted to foraging on the territory. I tried to duplicate these data in 1970. The curve followed the same upward trend, but at its peak I had to give up because the birds became too disturbed by my presence. What are the reasons for this difference in foraging pattern between males and females?

It is well known, certainly among Passerines, that older nestlings are more strongly defended than younger ones, which in their turn are more strongly defended than eggs. The explanation probably lies in an increasing social com-

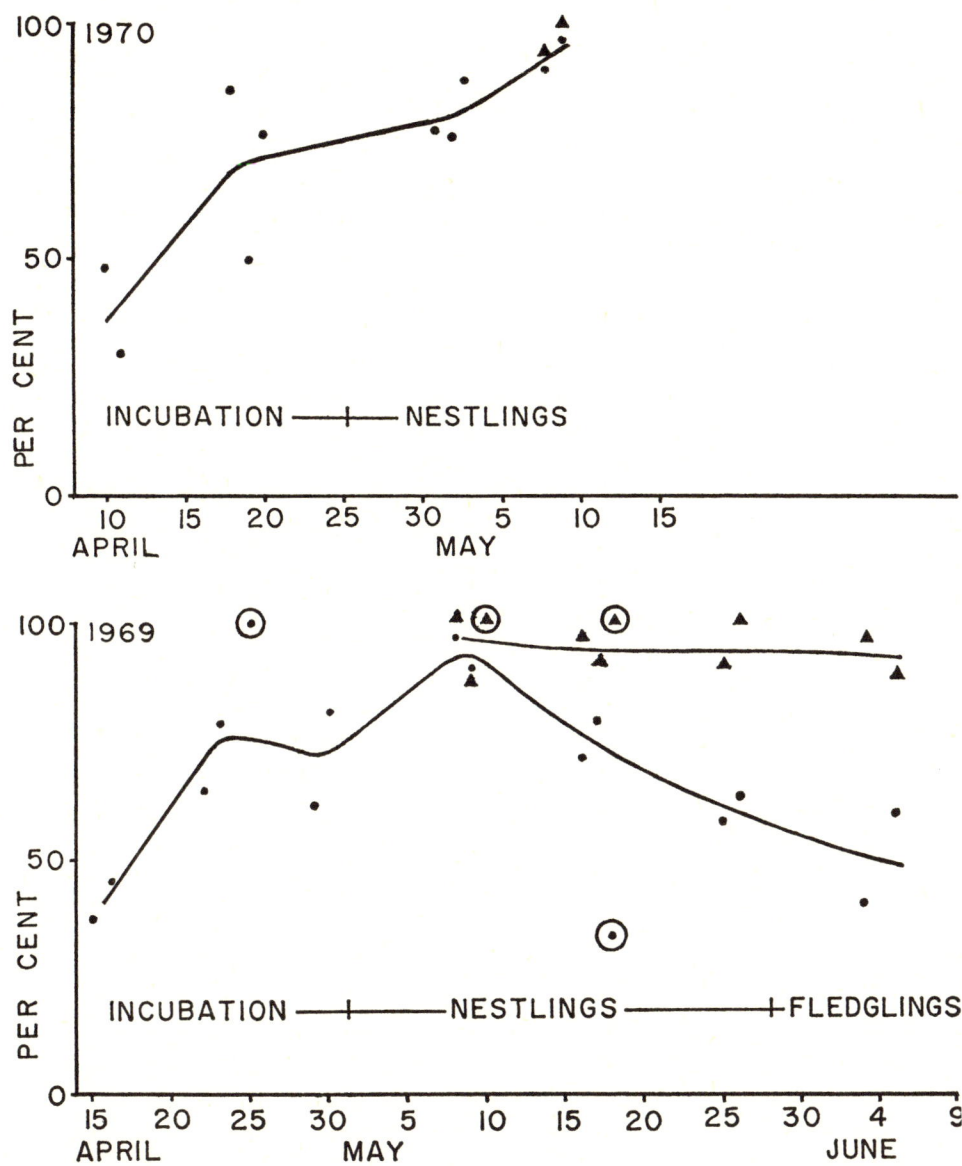

Fig. 11. Off-territory feedings as a percentage of all feedings (both on and off-territory). Male feedings (●), female feedings (▲). Small samples indicated by a circle.

mitment, largely brought about through movement and increasing vocal communication between parent and offspring. As male magpies are about 20 g heavier than females, one might argue that the larger sex stays closer to the nest to defend the young. However, in the Yellow-bill, and in the Black-bill (Erpino, 1968b), it is the female who does most of the mobbing. In the Yellow-bill this applies to both man and birds of prey. It thus seems unlikely that the male reverts to feeding on the territory to defend the nest. An alternate explanation is a matter of molt and energy expenditure. While incubating, the female expends relatively little energy as she is fed by the male on the nest. The male, on the other hand, almost doubles the time spent on flying and feeding. One male, early in incubation, flew about 12 km a day, but toward the end of incubation this increased to 25 km. Presumably this is a considerable expenditure of energy as magpies are not strong fliers. At the same time, and perhaps more important, the flight feathers begin to molt in the second week of May. Field evidence indicates that males begin to molt ahead of the females. Because the female is probably in better condition at this time and molts slightly later than the male, she is in better energetic balance; the male, however, has to slow down.

The birds keep close watch on each other's movements, so that in any given day all members of the colony obtain food for their young either from their own small territory or from a larger communal area (ca. 40 ha) surrounding the colony. If one bird happens to find a new feeding site, others will soon go there too. The shift is very sudden and conspicuous. The location of a new feeding area is communicated visually. If a bird repeatedly flies in a given direction, others will soon follow until all the birds go there. With a food supply that is locally abundant, such as the yearly outbreak of *Malacosoma*, this behavior is highly adaptive and must figure importantly in the colonial habit. If the birds were not colonial and had larger, exclusive territories, such as areas of 14—49 ha reported for *Corvus corone* (Wittenberg, 1968), then such favorable areas would be within the territorial boundaries of some pairs, who could not fully utilize the supply of food. Other pairs whose territories did not have locally abundant food supplies would attempt to forage in the territory of the more well-to-do neighbors, leading to much waste of time in territorial defense and reduced feeding rates because of long flight distances. In this situation nobody would do well. The alternative is a colonial system, with mutual exploitation of locally abundant food sources resulting from individual exploration. In his study of the Brewer Blackbird (*Euphagus cyanocephalus*) Horn (1968) comes to the same conclusion.

FLEDGLINGS

After fledging, the young stay in the nest tree for about 4–5 days before venturing out to neighboring trees. In the nest tree they remain silent except for the sound made while they clamber and flutter around, and their begging calls when the adults approach with food. Later they sit in more exposed places and utter the begging call at the sight of any adult. They will even beg for food from approaching siblings, other fledglings, and Acorn Woodpeckers (*Melanerpes formicivorus*). The inclusion of the woodpecker indicates that the fledglings appear to react to approaching black and white birds and have not yet learned to discriminate between those that bring food and those that do not. The adults apparently know their own offspring as I have never seen them feed strange young.

In the evening of about the sixth day after fledging the young are on the ground for the first time. There they peck at leaves, stones, and twigs and hold them briefly. They also hold objects under their feet at this time and peck at them. If a bird has an object in its bill one or more siblings will come over and try to take it or sometimes just look at it. Chases often result and the object usually ends up in the beaks of several of the young. The fledglings also nibble each other's bill, legs, and feathers rather frequently. From then on they spend more time on the ground, fly about more frequently, and often stray on neighboring territories, where they give rise to disputes among the adults and eventually withdraw. After about 10–14 days the young follow the parents to the area of the *Malacosoma* outbreak. In one case 46-day-old fledglings (counted from the day of hatching) were still fed by the parents; their begging was ignored when 55 days old. Total independence occurs about 49 days after hatching.

TABLE 8

FLEDGING SUCCESS OF THE YELLOW-BILLED MAGPIE

Year	No. of nests[1]	Extreme fledging dates	Median	\multicolumn{6}{c}{No. of fledglings}	Fledging success[2]
				0	1	2	3	4	5	
1968	7 (1)[3]	13 May–17 June	30 May	3	0	1	1	1	1	3.5
1969	5	20 May– 9 June	31 May	0	0	2	1	1	1	3.2
1970	7 (2)	22 May– 4 June	28 May	2	1	1	1	1	1	3.0
1971	12 (3)	18 May–26 May	23 May	9	1	1	1	0	0	2.0

[1]Total nests in the Hastings colony, not counting one nest in each year, except 1971, from whose young I obtained food samples (Verbeek, 1970).
[2]Based on nests that fledged at least one young.
[3]Nests of yearlings included in total number of nests shown.

Within the Hastings colony fledging dates spread out over 35 days in 1968, 20 days in 1969, 13 days in 1970, and 9 days in 1971. Fledging success, based on those nests that fledged at least one young, was highest in 1968 and lowest in 1971 (table 8). Considering all nests in the colony, 1969 was the most productive year with 3.2 young per nest fledged, and 1971 was the least productive with only 0.5 young per nest fledged. In 1968 two nests of adults were abandoned after incubation was well under way, and in 1970 one adult pair was robbed of its nestlings. In the dry and cool spring of 1971, nine nests were abandoned. In some of these I suspect that eggs were abandoned, but probably in most cases small nestlings were left to die. This was certainly the case in two nests that I was able to reach. Fledging success of the Black-billed Magpie in Montana is 3.4 per nest (Brown, 1957). I have found no comparative data in the European literature.

Early nests tend to fledge more young than later ones (table 9), possibly as a direct consequence of the increased flight distance to the food source and the steady reduction of food in general. Prior to May 18, 1968, most food, primarily adult *Tipula*, came from the territory or from a site 250 m from the center of the colony. On 19 May the birds began to exploit an outbreak of tent caterpillars located 950 m away on the other side of a ridge. To clear the ridge the birds had to rise about 90 m. The closer to this date the eggs hatched, the larger was the proportion of the food derived from the distant source. In 1969 and 1970 the tent caterpillar outbreak was first used on 14 May and 7 May respectively, at a site about 750 m away and an elevation of about 70 m above the colony. Aside from the longer flight distance, time spent in handling food is also longer because the Yellow-billed Magpie feeds almost exclusively on the pupae of this hairy caterpillar, and the pupae have to be extracted from their cocoons.

TABLE 9
FLEDGING DATES AND NUMBER OF YOUNG LEAVING THE NEST

1968	No. of young	1969	No. of young	1970	No. of young	1971	No. of young
13 May	4	20 May	2	22 May	5	20 May	1
25 May	5	26 May	5	24 May	1	23 May	3
3 June	2	30 May	4	31 May	4	26 May	2
17 June	3	1 June	3	3 June	2		
		9 June	2	4 June	3		

LIFE EXPECTANCY AND FLEDGLING SURVIVAL

In the Hastings colony about 15 percent of the breeding adults disappear and probably die before the next breeding season, assuming site tenacity. The four colonies within the study area have about 22 breeding pairs, and as the colonies remain rather stable this means that only about seven birds breeding for the first time are added to the population each year. On the basis of what might be considered normal years (1968 to 1970) these seven birds represent 10 to 16 percent of the young that fledged two years earlier. In a year of such low fledgling productivity as 1971, few if any young will likely survive to breed two years hence. On the other hand, the high productivity of 1969 probably led to a proportionately greater survival as reflected in the increased number of nests in 1971.

The annual death rate of 15 percent among adults indicates that once a bird is adult (2 years old) it has a mean life expectancy of about seven years, which means seven (potentially eight) reproductive years. In the Hastings colony at least three birds (B, BB, and WG) produced offspring in five consecutive years (1967 to 1971). All three birds were adult when banded in 1967.

INTERSPECIFIC INTERACTIONS WITH OTHER BIRDS

Throughout the year the Yellow-bill interacts with several species of hawks and corvids (fig. 12). The type of interaction depends on the size of the adversary and on the stage of the magpie breeding cycle. The Sparrow Hawk (*Falco sparverius*) seldom attacks magpies, but is at times mobbed by the latter. The Sharp-shinned Hawk (*Accipiter striatus*) is only mildly feared. Frequently when it chases a magpie the roles are reversed in mid-air with the magpie chasing the hawk. These two hawks are too small to catch magpies. The Cooper Hawk (*Accipiter cooperii*) is feared most and its presence causes great alarm. The adult magpies attack this hawk only when the magpie nestlings are about to fledge and after they have fledged. This hawk is capable of catching all age classes. The increase in interactions in late summer and fall between magpies and the Sharp-

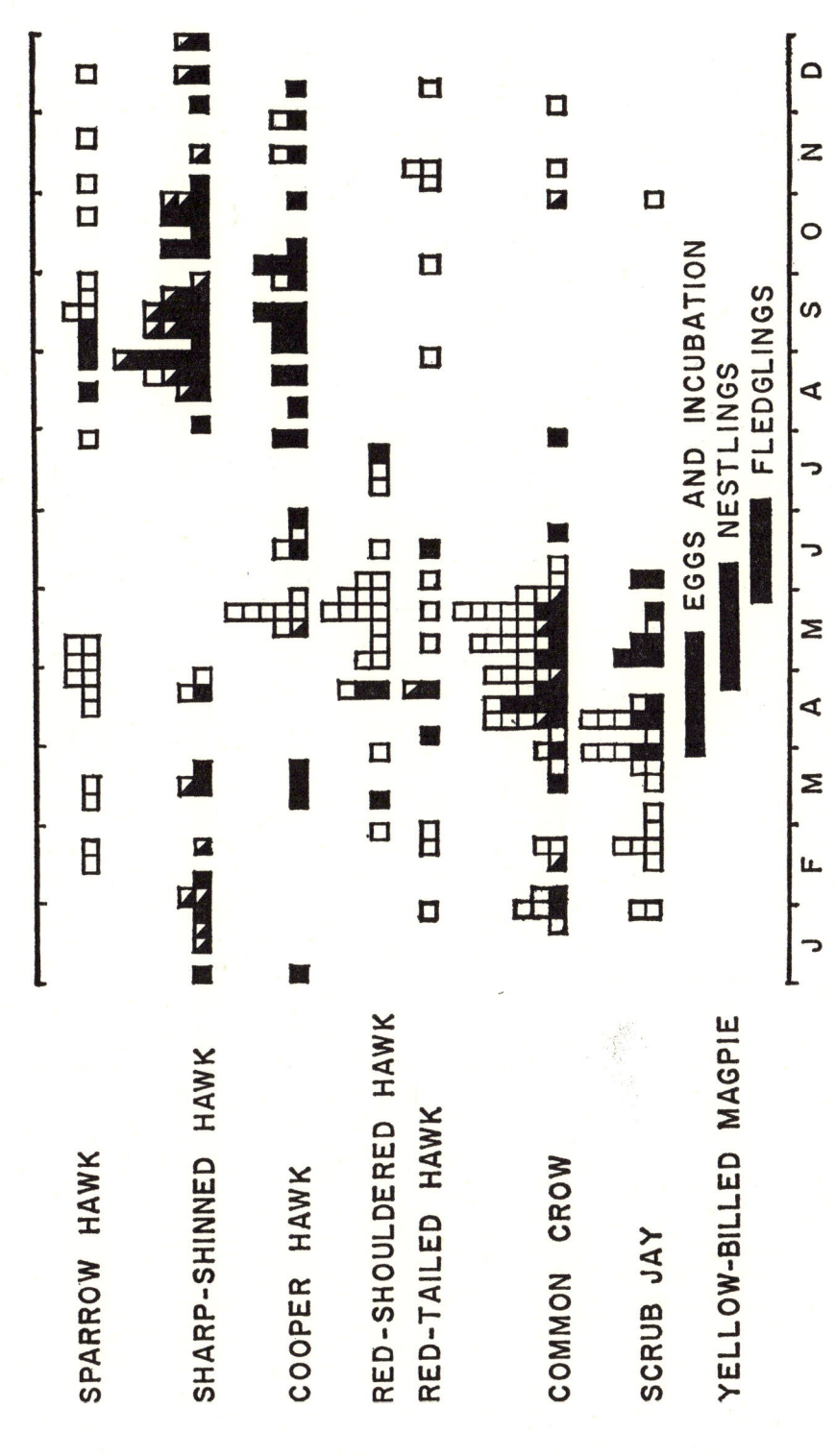

Fig. 12. Magpies attacking hawks and other corvids (white) and being attacked by them (black), in relation to the magpie nesting cycle. One square is one attack. Triangles indicate reciprocal attacks.

shinned and Cooper Hawks is due to immature birds and an influx of migrating Sharp-shins. Of the two Buteos, the Red-tailed Hawk (*Buteo jamaicensis*) shows little interest in magpies except during the nesting season. Tomich (fieldnotes) found two feathers of a fledgling magpie under a Red-tail's nest. Infrequently through the year this hawk is mobbed by the magpies. Red-shouldered Hawks (*Buteo lineatus*) and magpies interact only when the latter have nestlings and fledglings. I saw this hawk take the nestlings from the nests of two Scrub Jays and one Black-headed Grosbeak (*Pheucticus melanocephalus*) in 1969.

Most of the year Common Crows, Yellow-bills, and Scrub Jays show no overt aggression toward each other and at times feed near each other. During the nesting season this relationship changes; the aggression is then limited to the nest and territory. A crow robbed a Scrub Jay's nest of eggs in 1969, and magpie–crow interactions also peak at the time the magpie nests contain eggs and nestlings (fig. 12). Brown (1957) reports that 12 of 731 nests of the Black-bill lost their eggs to Common Crow predation. In Europe, Carrion Crows (Brown, 1924) and Hooded Crows (*Corvus cornix*, Holyoak, 1967) rob magpie nests. Interactions of the Scrub Jay and the magpie are of a different nature. Because of the prolonged nest-building period of the magpie, it begins to chase the jay in late January whenever it comes close to the magpie nest. The Scrub Jay does not start to build until late March and its aggressiveness to the magpie does not appear until that time. The Golden Eagle (*Aquila chrysaëtos*) takes nestling and fledgling Yellow-bills (Carnie, 1954) and Black-bills (no age specified, McGahan, 1968). In Europe the Goshawk (*Accipiter gentilis*) robs nests of the Black-bill (Steinfatt, 1943; pers. obs.).

FLOCKING

To discuss flocking one has to distinguish among age classes, as in other phases of the annual cycle. Once the fledglings are capable of sustained flight over short distances, the family moves away from the territory during the day to the current best feeding area. In the Hastings colony, during the four seasons of this study, this was an area about 800 m to the southeast, where tent caterpillars were the major food source. When other families in the colony matured they, too, frequented this area. At first each family stays together as a unit, but the tendency to flock collectively is already present. When one family moves to another part of the feeding area, the others soon drift in that direction, too. With further independence of the young the individual families begin to break up. Yearlings, which have continued to flock in small groups in the general neighborhood ever since the previous year, join this combined family flock. By late June members of several colonies join together, along with the yearlings, and the largest flocks occur in July and August (fig. 13).

Most of the birds in the summer flock are produced locally, but there is also a visible movement of birds into and out of the study area. These are presumed to be young of the year, because adults and yearlings are strongly attached to the local area and their respective colonies. The rapid decline of flock size in late summer (fig. 13) indicates a steady exodus of young birds at that time. It should be kept in mind that figure 13 depicts flock size and not the total number of birds in the study area. Only in July and August, when the flock is largest, does it

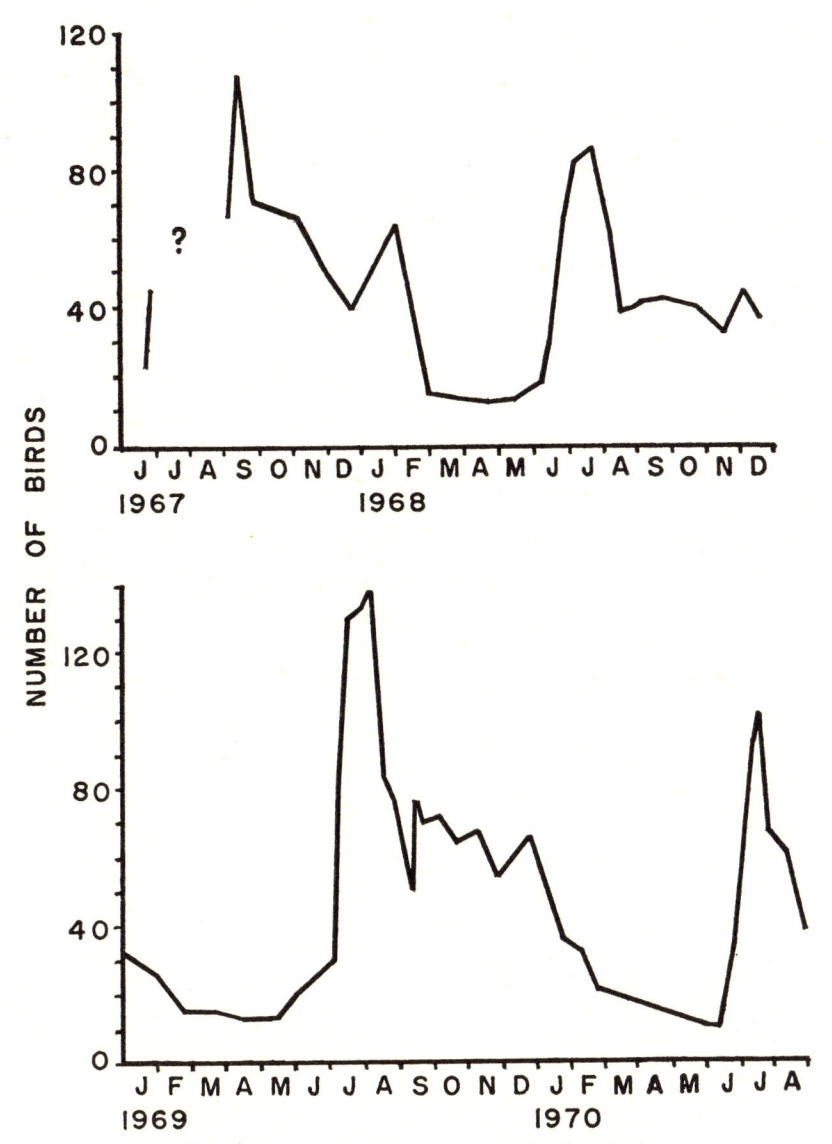

Fig. 13. Seasonal changes in size of feeding flock.

closely represent all the birds in the study area (fig. 2). From September onward the flock breaks up, but it may reassemble again, as was seen by a sudden increase in January 1968, apparently the result of a snowstorm. The flock size steadily declines toward the breeding season. In the fall and early winter adults and yearlings flock together during the day, but this flock becomes smaller as more and more adults spend more time near their respective colonies. From the end of February to early March adults and yearlings no longer flock together, although they may feed in the same area. During the breeding season only the yearlings flock (fig. 14).

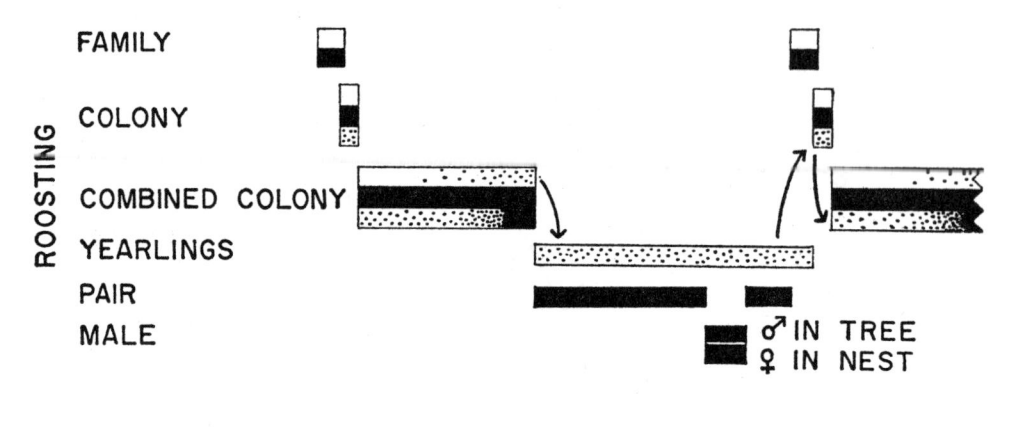

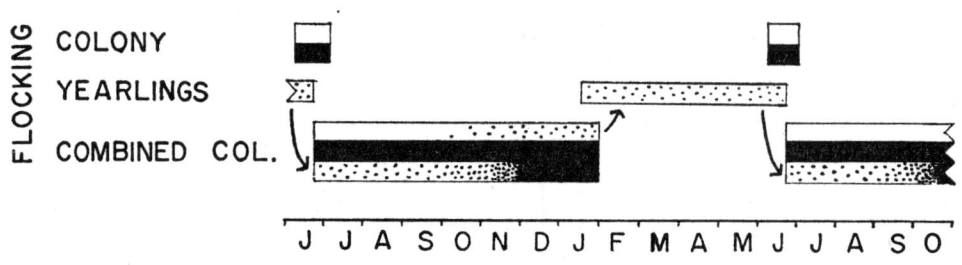

Fig. 14. Seasonal changes in roosting and flocking. Juveniles (white), yearlings (stipple), adults (black).

The maximum range of color-banded adults during the summer is about 3.5 km from the Hastings colony. One yearling bird was recovered 5 km to the northwest of the Hastings colony.

Annually, the birds spend more time on grazed pasture, where the grass is shorter, than on the Reservation. Besides providing cow pats, the cattle also change the grassland by grazing and trampling, making it easier for the magpies to search for food. Invertebrates hidden under dry cow pats are a rich food source for magpies (Verbeek, 1970). The periodic absences of Yellow-bills from the Reservation for parts of June, July, and August are related to inaccessibility and scarcity of food and not to the need for moister areas closer to the coast (Linsdale, 1946, p. 179). Throughout the summer magpies are present on grazed pasture at higher and drier altitudes 3 km to the southeast of the Reservation. Even though food is scarce and inaccessible in dry years, such as in the summer of 1968, when the magpies were absent from the Reservation for only 7 days in June and July, the birds have to come to the Reservation for drinking water. In the summer of 1967, with abundant rainfall in late spring, the birds probably found natural sources of water elsewhere, and were absent from the Reservation for 49 days.

The daily foraging beat is not very predictable, but when the birds use a new area for the first time they are likely to go there again the next day. The same is true of the choice of a roosting site as discussed below. Early in the wandering phase, when several water sources, both man-made and natural, are still available, the foraging beat leads to these in the early mid-morning and again in the late afternoon. Later on, when only a few cattle troughs provide water, the birds often have to interrupt their foraging beat to fly as much as a kilometer for water.

ROOSTING

The analysis of roosting in the Yellow-bill is complicated because there are three age classes, seasonal differences in sociality, and seasonal changes in roosting sites. This results in six types of roost (fig. 14), varying in size from one for a single male when the female is incubating to one that will hold as many as 150 birds or more during the summer. This multiplicity of roosts is reported also for *Cyanopica cyana* (Hosono, 1967) and for *Corvus corone* (Wittenberg, 1968) but is probably more widespread among flocking corvids.

The six types of roosts break down into two categories. The roosts of the individual pairs, the male, and the family are associated with the territory. Colony roosts, combining breeding adults, young, and yearlings, are not associated with the territory. As the range of the Hastings colony extends as far as 3 km, all of the non-territorial roosts (fig. 14) are within the home range, except for the School Hill roost (fig. 3). Linsdale (1946, p. 176) refers to the School Hill roost as being outside the daytime range of the magpies, but this is only because there happens to be no open grassland surrounding this roost, as is the case with the Haystack roost. The distinction of roosts into those located within or outside of the home range, as reported for *Cyanopica cyana* (Hosono, 1967), does not apply to *Pica nuttalli*.

Linsdale (1946) reports on roosting behavior at length and little needs to be added. The birds roost almost exclusively in the inner canopy of live oaks. In spite of careful watching I have never seen magpies roosting in nests as reported for the Black-bill by Erpino (1968b), except for the female, who sleeps in the nest as soon as it contains the first egg. Before entering the roost the birds gather in one or more trees at some distance from the actual roost. If the flock is large, some reshuffling occurs as individuals bicker about perches. The birds are very cautious when entering and leaving the roost. The least irregularity, especially disturbing or strange noises, such as the warning calls of Acorn Woodpeckers (*Melanerpes formicivorus*) or the sound of a person whistling, is enough to scatter the flock or delay its departure for the roost. When not disturbed and at the proper light intensity (fig. 4) the first birds fly to the roost in small groups, followed a little later by the main flock and finally the last stragglers. Large flocks tend to roost earlier and rise earlier than small flocks or single pairs. Often the birds will gather once more in tall trees at the roost itself, and when all appears safe, dive erratically into the roosting trees below. In the morning the procedure is the same in reversed order.

Pair Roost on the Territory

In the second half of October the adult pairs begin to abandon the combined roost, leaving the yearlings, and roost on their territories. The switch from the combined to the territorial roost is a slow process. At first only one or two pairs, or even one member of a pair, roost on their territory and after one or more days they may temporarily rejoin the yearlings. By the middle of December the change-over is completed.

Before flying into their roost the individual pairs sit conspicuously in the very top of a tree within or near the territory. At first several trees may serve this function, but as territories expand towards the breeding season, some of these trees may become incorporated into the territories of other pairs. The conspicuousness of this behavior serves to indicate one's presence and claim to that territory, and not to defend the nest against Sparrow Hawks as suggested by Linsdale (1946), as magpies are quite capable of routing this hawk.

Usually there are only one or two roosting trees. Once nest-building is well under way the tendency is to roost closer to the nest tree, but this depends on the proximity of a live oak. Whereas the pair sometimes roosts in the future nest tree, they do not use that tree once the nest is being built unless it is a live oak and the territory has no other live oak available. In the tree the birds sit close together on the same branch. When flying into the roost the male usually goes first (silently) followed by the female who usually calls a nervous *key-keck*.

MALE ROOST

Once the first egg is laid and until the nestlings are no longer brooded at night, the female spends the night on the nest, leaving the male to roost alone. Some males appear reluctant to roost alone and they may roost in the nest tree for one or two nights, but after that they will roost elsewhere on the territory, usually in the same tree as was used by the pair earlier. Single males tend to roost later with respect to light intensity than when roosting with their mates. They also remain silent when they fly into the roost, making it difficult to see when and where they roost, unless one watches an individual closely.

FAMILY ROOST

After fledging, the young roost in the nest tree if it happens to be a live oak, while the adults continue to roost in the tree they used prior to fledging of the young. In one instance of a nest in a locust (*Robinia pseudoacacia*) when no live oak was within reach of the limited flight ability of the fledglings, the young spent the first four nights in the nest. Whether fledglings in live oaks also spend the night in the nest is uncertain, as visibility is minimal at dusk. During this early period the adults coax the fledglings back to the nest tree or the nest if the young have strayed away during the day.

Of five nests observed, the young roosted alone for 3, 5, 5, 9, and 10 days, the variability depending on the distance between the nest tree and the adult roost and the presence of intervening trees that could be used to bridge the gap. In the case where it took 10 days, the gap was about 100 m. Following this short period of separate roosting sites, the family sleeps together in the usual roosting tree of the adults.

This system of separate roosts has probably evolved as an anti-predator device. The young are clumsy fliers, noisy, and easily frightened, and could thus attract the attention of predators. Killpack (1951) and Brown (1957) report predation by

Great Horned Owls (*Bubo virginianus*) on fledgling Black-billed Magpies. The tendency to avoid roosting with the young is seen at times after the young are capable of crossing the gap between roosts. One pair, on being joined by the young for the first time, flew out of the tree after the young had quieted down, even though the adults had roosted there for the past months. They were joined moments later by two of the fledglings and by then it was too dark to shift again. Another time, a female led five fledglings (37 days old) into a tree. Afterwards she flew out of the tree to a nearby telephone wire, where she was joined by two of the fledglings. She again flew to the tree followed by the young. After the latter had settled down, the female flew to the wire and from there to a tree 100 m away where she roosted.

COLONY ROOST

With improvement of the flight capabilities of the fledglings and further breakdown of territories, family groups tend to roost near each other but still as family units. Yearlings may join this roost or they may in turn be joined by the families. During the day the families move away, more or less as separate units, to the common feeding ground. If this feeding ground is rather far away the birds may not return to the colony for several days but roost close to the feeding area. As flight improves they usually return to the home colony to roost. On the Reservation this roost was located on the edge of the colony and coincided with the earlier roost of two of the adult pairs.

COMBINED COLONY ROOST

When the fledglings become independent the wandering phase begins. Members of several colonies flock during the day and roost together at night. This roost is maintained until about early December, when the adults have completed their change-over to the territory roost and only the yearlings remain together.

Because of high mid-day temperatures in summer and early fall the birds feed primarily in the early morning and late afternoon and hold a siesta in between (Verbeek, 1972). This siesta is longest in July and August and it forces the birds to feed intensely until shortly before going to roost. During this time of the year the foraging beat leads directly to one of the regular roosts, and the birds fly directly into it from the ground without spending time in a pre-roost tree. Occasionally in July and August the flock finds itself away from a traditional roost, and because of late feeding and reluctance to fly at dusk, the birds will roost opportunistically, even in trees other than live oaks. Usually, such opportunistic roosts are used only once. Because they feed late and are reluctant to fly, the birds stay together at roosting time. Thus the largest roosts are found in July and August. Between the end of August and early September, because of decreasing daytime temperatures, the siesta is slightly shorter and the birds stop feeding earlier. This allows them to fly to a more distant traditional roost and to choose a particular one. This is shown by a break-up of the flock at roosting time, some birds going to the School Hill roost (fig. 3) others to the Pond roost. The core birds in these roosts are the adults and yearlings belonging to the nearby colony (i.e., Hastings colony adults roost on School Hill; Pond and Mill colony adults roost in the Pond roost). The adults are joined by varying numbers of juveniles. In the transition period any one of these roosts may be abandoned for several nights in a row, but by mid-September at least the adults and yearlings are present. This arrangement continues until the adults and yearlings shift to their territorial roost, leaving the juveniles.

ROOST OF THE YEARLINGS

During the following 7 months (October–June) the yearlings roost together. The site may be separate from the adults' or it may coincide with one or more territories of adults. In the winters of 1967 and 1968 they roosted separate from the adults at the Pond roost. In late fall to early winter 1968 four yearlings used a roost on School Hill close to the Hastings colony, and their presence attracted one adult pair from the colony to roost there, too, during this period. In the fall of 1969, 36 yearlings continued to roost on School Hill after the adults had withdrawn to their territories. In the first week of December they switched to the Hastings colony and began to roost in the middle of it. They occupied a few trees located on two territories and continued to roost there in decreasing numbers until 17 March. With such an overwhelming number of trespassers the territory owners could do little to evict them. At roosting time the birds were uncommonly noisy, and it was not clear whether this was because of the eviction attempts of the adults or because there were too many birds and too few suitable branches to sleep on to maintain proper distance between sleeping pairs. I suspect the former. The adults avoided sleeping with the yearlings by waiting until they had settled down. Then they would fly to a live oak on their territory not occupied by the yearlings.

MOLT

The timing of molt in relation to the breeding cycle and the food supply is of considerable ecological interest. In the context of this paper a detailed study of pterylography and molt was considered unnecessary. Details of pterylography of *Pica pica* are provided by Lowe (1938), Burckhardt (1954), and Bock (1962). Adult and yearling Yellow-billed Magpies have only one complete annual molt. This applies also to the Black-billed Magpie (Bährmann, 1968), and is typical of corvids (Dwight, 1900; Pitelka, 1945). The post-juvenile molt is incomplete and does not involve the flight feathers.

Stages in molt were scored with the system devised by Pitelka (1958) for the Steller Jay (*Cyanocitta stelleri*). At a score of 70, adult molt is essentially completed, while a score of 50 indicates completion of the post-juvenile molt. In the Yellow-bill, adult molt overlaps in part with the nestling period and begins at a time when food is still abundant (fig. 15). Most of the molt in adults and young, however, occurs in summer, when invertebrate food is relatively scarce. From its inception to completion, individual molt requires about 4.5 months in adults and about 3.5 months in juveniles. Although the food supply is relatively low, high ambient temperatures decrease energy requirements for self-maintenance. Surplus energy can thus be channeled to meet the demands for molting. This has also been argued for Clark's Nutcracker (*Nucifraga columbiana*) (Mewaldt, 1958). As juveniles do not replace the flight feathers, they molt more quickly. Comparison of the timing of molt of the Yellow-bill with other corvids, and its ecological significance, are discussed later.

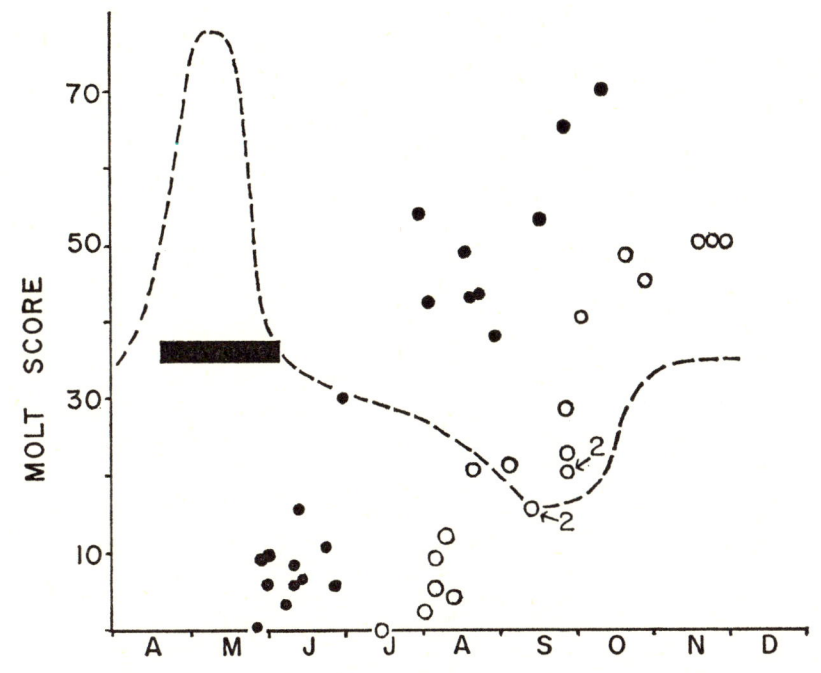

Fig. 15. Period of molt in adult (closed circles) and juvenile (open circles) Yellow-billed Magpies. The black bar indicates period when nestlings are present. The dashed line represents a generalized picture of invertebrate food abundance.

DISCUSSION

The major behavioral features of the exploitation system of the Yellow-billed Magpie and the Scrub Jay are compared in table 10. Considering the timing of certain events, three are of particular interest—timing of the breeding season, molt, and flocking.

Dates of the first Yellow-billed Magpie eggs on the Hastings Reservation fell within a period of three weeks. Higher spring temperatures apparently cause breeding to start earlier, within certain limitations. Starting too early could be as dysgenic as starting too late; thus, temperature alone is not all-important as a signal to begin the breeding cycle. A certain synchrony between the magpie and the Scrub Jay indicates that each independently responds to similar favorable signals. The Scrub Jay on the average laid its eggs a week earlier than the Yellow-billed Magpie. The breeding season is generally believed to be timed so that food availability will be at a maximum at the time the nestlings are in the nest (Lack, 1954).

To ascertain the importance of food in the timing of the breeding effort, I assessed the insect fauna (see Methods) in 1969, 1970, and 1971. The details are presented elsewhere (Verbeek, 1970) and summarized in figure 16. To the casual observer most food is available in May and early June when the standing crop of new vegetation is highest (fig. 6). The invertebrate fauna can be divided into two large assemblages: the cryptozoa and soil fauna (mainly earthworms), and the

TABLE 10

A Comparison of *Pica nuttalli* and *Aphelocoma coerulescens*

	Yellow-billed Magpie	Scrub Jay
Habitat	Grassland, savanna	Chaparral, woodland
Local population units		
Breeding	Colonies of 5–7 pairs	Settled pairs
Non-breeding	Coalesced colony flocks up to 140 individuals	Settled pairs, yearling flocks up to 30 birds
Home range size		
Breeding	About 40 ha	About 3 ha
Non-breeding	About 600 ha	About 3 ha
Territory size	About 1 ha	About 3 ha
Territory defense	All year, most strongly during breeding season	Intense, year round
Territory function	Nest material, some food, roosting	All necessities
Pair bond	Life	Life
Age at first breeding	Second year, a few first year	First or second year
Courtship feeding	During egg laying and incubation	Prior to egg laying through incubation
Copulation	Stolen copulations common	Stolen copulations not seen
Weight of adult ♀	145.5 g (N = 15)	85.9 g (N = 9)
Egg weight	8.3 g (N = 8)[1]	6.0 g (N = 11)
Nest height	16.9 m (9–24) N = 29	1.6 m (0.7–2.3) N = 25
Nest construction period	About 10 weeks	About 1.5 weeks
Nest weight	11,270 g (N = 1)	214 g (N = 4)
Distance between nests	31 m (7–44) N = 12	135 m (85–182) N = 5
Nest type	Domed	Open
Helpers at the nest	None	None
Clutch size	6.5 (5–8) Modal 7 N = 70[1]	3.9 (2–5) Modal 4 N = 29
First egg dates[2]	26 March–19 April, median 7 April N = 12	23 March–9 April, median 1 April N = 9
Incubation period	18 days	17–18 days
Hatching	Asynchronous	Asynchronous
Nestling period	28 days (25–31) N = 8	20–24 days, N = 2[3]
Nestling dates[2]	19 April–9 June, median 14 May N = 12	13 April–21 May, median 2 May N = 8
Mean length of nestling food[4]	13.88 mm (3–40) N = 2401	15.36 mm (3–50) N = 995
Young brooded	16 days	Period unknown
Fledgling care[5]	Independent at 49 days	Fed until at least 74 days
Fledging period[2]	20 May–9 June, median 30 May N = 12	10 May–21 May, median 16 May N = 7
Flocking	All age classes after breeding season	Immatures only
Roosting	Complex with seasonal shifts	On territory
Adult molt	Middle May to end October	Begin June to end October
Post-juvenal molt	Middle July to middle November	End June to end October

[1] Based on Linsdale, 1937.
[2] Based on 1969 and 1970.
[3] Nestling periods of 18 days reported in the literature are doubtful.
[4] Invertebrates only.
[5] Counted from the day of hatching.

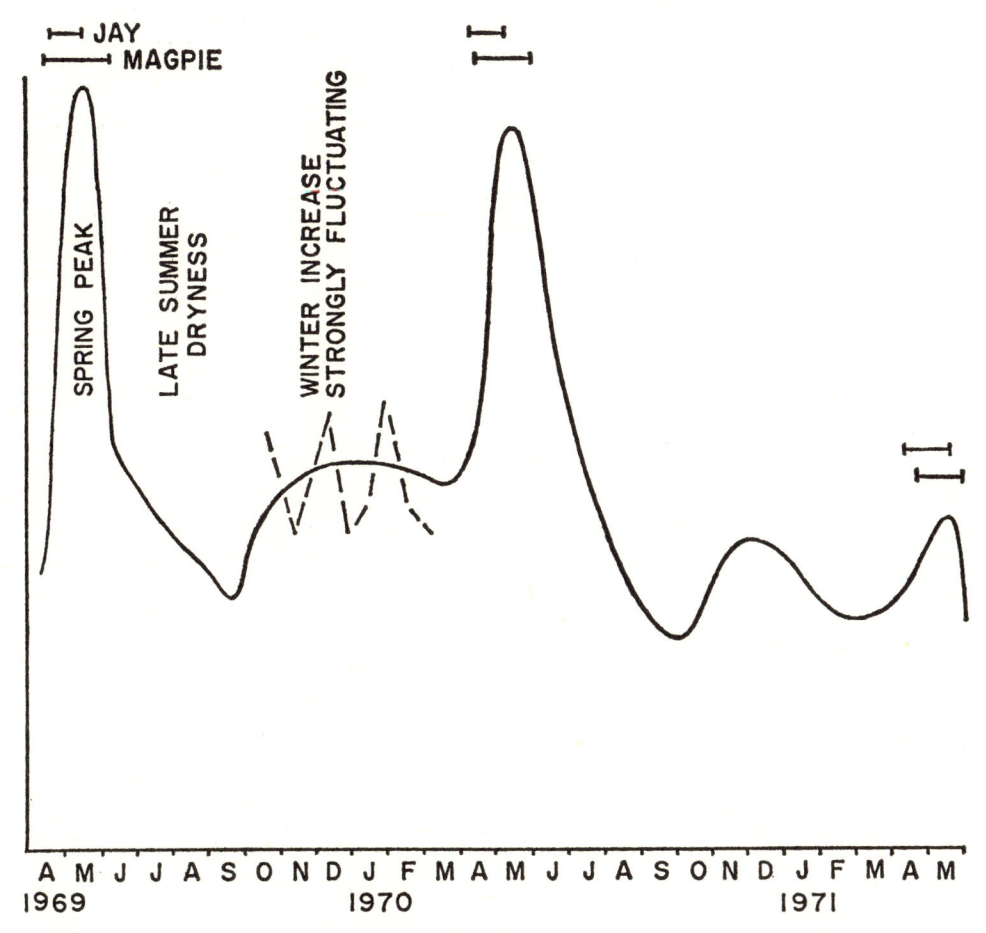

Fig. 16. Relative abundance of invertebrate prey in relation to the nestling period of the Yellow-billed Magpie and the Scrub Jay. Greater fluctuations in the winter season are indicated by the dashed line.

aboveground fauna. The former decline (increasing dryness) when the latter increase, so that in May and early June food variety is greatest. To some extent the reverse situation occurs when the rainy season begins in October.

Figure 16 shows two major and three minor peaks in food abundance, seemingly obscuring the importance of food supply in the timing of the breeding season. Two of the minor peaks occur in the autumn and winter months. Invertebrate abundance in the autumn builds up soon after the first fall rains, following a long summer drought (table 1). In both years these rains brought to the surface an increasing number of cryptozoa (primarily earwigs, isopods, and a small species of carabid) and small caterpillars. The increase in invertebrate abundance in the autumn and winter of 1969 was accompanied by strong fluctuations. For instance, the narrow peak in February resulted from an increase in spiders (*Lycosa*) stimulated by unusually warm February temperatures. Such strong fluctuations were not evident in the autumn peak of 1970, perhaps because of less frequent censusing, nor did this peak maintain itself as in 1969. This was largely because of an early decline of caterpillars and a lack of spiders in January and February. The autumn peaks appear to be formed by a fauna that lacks diversity and whose members show strong fluctuations in numbers.

The three remaining peaks occurred in May of each year and coincided with the mean nestling dates. The spring peaks of 1969 and 1970 were maintained over a relatively long period and showed no internal fluctuations, only a steady build-up of invertebrates. The slightly weaker fit of the nestling period with maximum food abundance in 1970 was due to an early dry season. No rain fell between 11 March and 13 April. This produced an earlier withdrawal of the cryptozoa. In 1971 vertebrate abundance was lower in the late winter and early spring than in the same period in 1970. In addition, the expected spring peak in 1971 did not materialize. Several of the usual staples failed to appear (*Tipula* sp.), appeared in insignificant numbers (thomisid spiders), or were delayed (*Malacosoma* pupae, Orthoptera). Low food levels during the incubation and nestling periods resulted in a large-scale failure of the breeding effort (table 8), because nestlings, and presumably also eggs, were abandoned. It appears that the Yellow-billed Magpie times the period that its nestlings are in the nest rather closely to peak food abundance and that this timing is crucial within narrow limits.

Analysis of food brought to the nestling Yellow-billed Magpies and Scrub Jays shows that these two species exploit a wide variety of food, and that there is considerable overlap (Verbeek, 1970). The invertebrate prey ranged in size from 3 to 50 mm in the jay and from 3 to 40 mm in the magpie. In the Scrub Jay 40–50 percent of the nestling diet was lepidopterous larvae. The magpie is less specialized, although 35 percent of its nestling diet consisted of Lepidoptera. Of these, 65 percent were pupae and 35 percent were larvae. The Scrub Jay's greater concentration on larvae may account for its earlier mean nestling period. In addition, courtship feeding in advance of egg laying provides the female with extra food to form eggs earlier. In the Scrub Jay the weight of the total clutch is only 27 percent of the female body weight, in contrast to 37 percent in the magpie (table 10). Both species, especially the magpie, are also very opportunistic, concentrating on whatever prey species are most abundant in any one year. This opportunism thwarted efforts to census more specifically for those food items likely to be important in any given year. Several of these were not censused by the techniques I used because they occurred in areas which were not part of the regular census beat and which often shifted from year to year. In figure 17 I have graphed some of the major food items censused in 1969 in areas where they were densest and where the magpies concentrated. *Malacosoma* pupae, for instance, formed about 21 percent of all food brought to the nestlings. The timing of the breeding cycle to this locally abundant food is much more apparent in figure 17 than one would conclude from figure 16, which merely shows ecological density of top-soil and surface invertebrates generally.

Figure 18 shows the length of molt from inception to completion for the first adult and fledgling magpie of the season. Included are similar data for the Scrub Jay and the Steller Jay (Pitelka, 1945, 1958). In the adult Yellow-billed Magpie the complete molt begins earlier than in the much smaller Scrub Jay. In the magpie it overlaps with the end of the nestling period, in the Scrub Jay the two phases

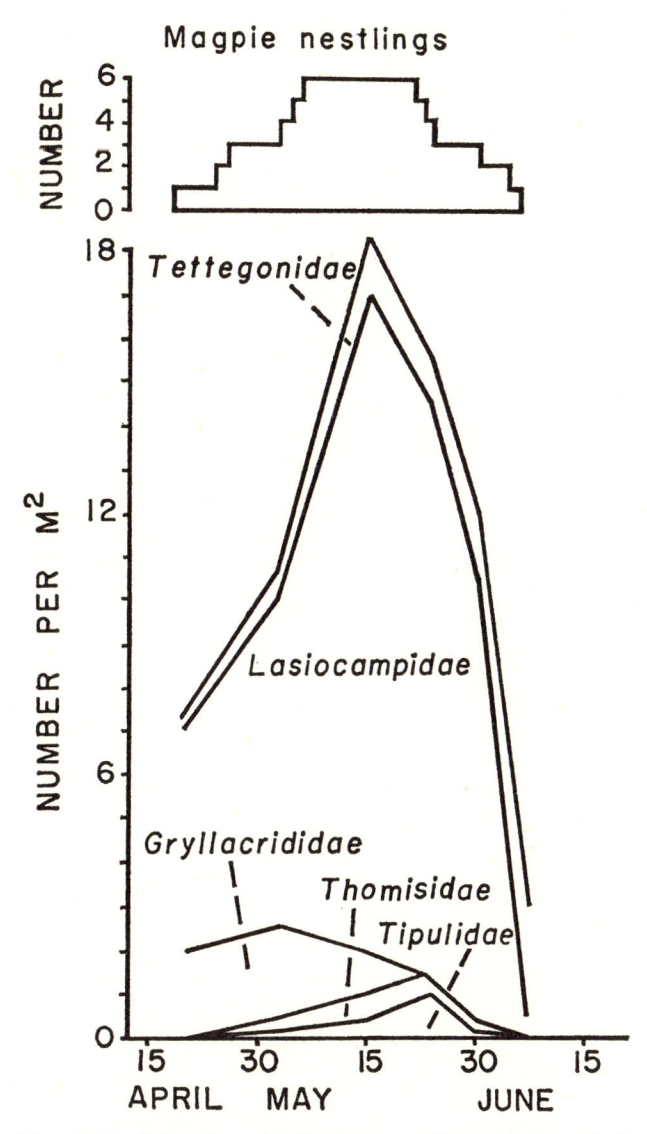

Fig. 17. Food abundance in relation to nestling period graphed cumulatively. The data are from the 1969 nesting season.

are well separated. Contrarily, the post-juvenile molt in the Scrub Jay begins much earlier than in the magpie. Both age classes of the Scrub Jay complete their molt before the magpies do. The difference between the adult magpie and Scrub Jay might be in part related to the longer period of dependence of the fledgling jays on the parents. The extra food the former receive allows them to molt earlier and this delays the molt of the parents.

Pitelka (1958) argues that in the Steller Jay of colder northern latitudes the period of molt has evolved to overlap more with peak food abundance, thus com-

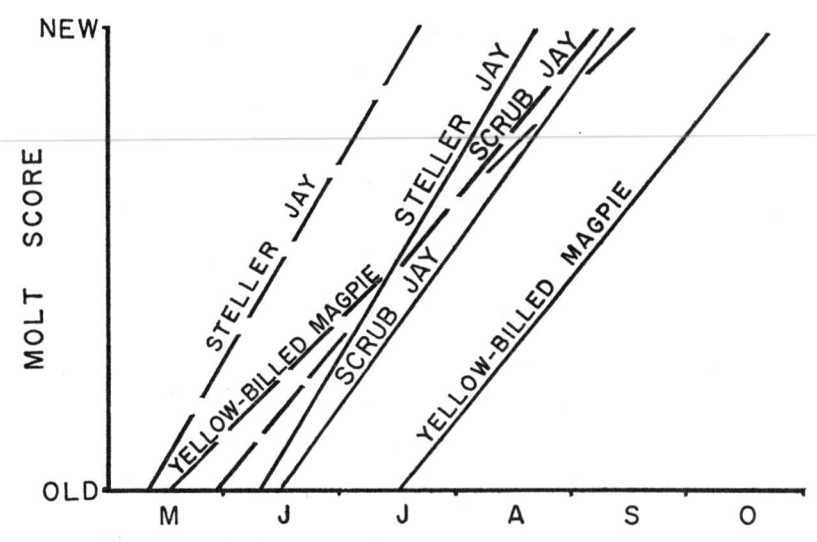

Fig. 18. Inception and completion of molt in adults (dashed line) and juveniles (solid line) in three corvids. For clarity of the figure only the first bird to start and complete its molt is shown. Data on Scrub Jay and Steller Jay after Pitelka 1945, 1958.

promising the basic timing of the nestling period in its relation to the food peak. The periods of molt in adult and juvenile birds only partly overlap, so that the demand on the food supply at any one time is reduced. This latter point certainly also applies to the Yellow-billed Magpie but not to the Scrub Jay for reasons suggested earlier. Regarding Pitelka's earlier point, the magpie does not molt at a time of peak food abundance, assuming that figure 15 depicts the true nature of the invertebrate food supply. The food supply of the Scrub Jay was not assessed, except in so far as it overlaps with that of the magpie. However, abundance of foliage arthropods also peaks in May and decreases throughout the summer (Root, 1967). Both species thus molt at a time of reduced food abundance, resulting in a slower rate of molt, more pronounced in the magpie than in the Scrub Jay. The Scrub Jay has a wider repertoire of feeding styles and occupies a wider feeding niche that includes trees, woodland and scrub floor, and grassland. This might give it an advantage over the magpie, allowing it to molt in a shorter period, and also allowing it to occupy self-contained territories in the first place. The Scrub Jays of the interior of California and Arizona have a longer period of molt and a wider gap between the period of molt in adults and fledglings (Pitelka, 1945) than do coastal populations. This is probably related to harsher food conditions in the interior, and in these populations we might expect even longer periods of fledgling dependence on the parents.

Flocking is widespread among corvids. In those species that do not normally breed until their second year (which probably includes most corvids) small, loosely constructed flocks of first-year birds roam about until they begin to breed for the first time (*Pyrrhocorax*, Mayaud, 1933; *Corvus*, Wittenberg, 1968; *Cyanocitta*, Hardy, 1961; *Aphelocoma*, Brown, 1963a; *Cyanocorax*, Crossin, 1967; *Pica*, this study; and others). In some species these flocks are later joined by the breeding adults and young of the year. The cases where adults do not join the flocks all involve species with type A territories (Hinde, 1956), such as *Perisoreus canadensis* (Rutter, 1969), *Corvus coronoides* (Rowley, 1967), *Corvus capensis* (Skead, 1952), *Aphelocoma coerulescens* (this study). In species with type B territories, such as *Corvus mellori* (Rowley, 1967) and *Pica nutalli* (this study), adults and young of the year join the yearlings and roam together for some variable time. The difference between these two systems appears to be related to some feature(s) of the territory, presumably food.

At the Hastings Reservation I saw the earliest flock of Scrub Jays (30 birds) on 28 August. Smaller flocks were present at the next breeding season. These birds occupy woodland or chaparral away from the edge where the adults hold territories. In this species juveniles remain on the parental territories until they are independent. Independence is delayed as indicated by the prolonged period of parental care. The exclusive territory is apparently rich enough in food to support the family for that length of time. In the Yellow-bill combined flocking starts at the end of June when the young of the year are independent, thus well in advance of the Scrub Jay. Continued dependence of fledglings on parents is difficult in a flock situation. The magpie territory is too small to support the family until the middle of August. This is also apparent as parents take their young off the territory to better feeding areas, once they are able to fly but before they are totally independent. The largest flocks of feeding Yellow-bills are encountered in July and August (fig. 13).

Although the literature abounds with data concerning sizes of corvid roosts, comparative data for sizes of feeding assemblages are lacking. Size of feeding flocks cannot simply be equated with size of roosts, as the latter are frequently occupied by several feeding flocks that come from and disperse to different areas. We may, however, say that size of roosts generally reflects size of feeding assemblages. This holds true for the Yellow-bill, where in mid-summer the largest number of birds in the roost coincides with the largest feeding assemblage. Later in the winter, feeding assemblages are larger than any one roost, because of the complex nature of roosting behavior at that time. In areas with cold winters, the largest roosts of corvids occur in the winter (*Corvus brachyrhynchos*, Haase, 1963; *Corvus monedula* and *C. cornix*, Borgvall, 1952; *Corvus frugilegus*, Bent, 1946, in England, but not in Poland, where the species is migratory, Pinowski, 1959; and *Cyanopica cyana*, Hosono, 1967). The timing of flocking thus coincides with that time of the year when food conditions are severe. In open areas with good visibility, once a good food source has been located, feeding birds can be easily spotted by others who have not yet found food. Pinowski (1959) showed this clearly in his study of *Corvus frugilegus*. Corvids that gather in large flocks to feed or roost are all species that inhabit open country.

The variety of ecological and behavioral strategies in birds, and the adaptive significances inherent in them, have been set out by Crook (1965), Lack (1968), and Tinbergen (1967). The general conclusion is that nesting dispersion and feeding dispersion are influenced by two factors: the distribution and abundance of food, and predator avoidance. Nesting dispersions are of four types: solitary,

TABLE 11
NEST DISPERSION OF SPECIES OF CORVIDAE IN RELATION TO HABITAT

Habitat	Genus or species	Solitary	Loosely colonial	Colonial
Forest				
Coniferous..................	*Nucifraga, Perisoreus*	4		
Coniferous and deciduous....	*Cyanocitta stelleri*			
	Garrulus glandarius	1		
Woodland				
Hardwood..................	*Cyanocitta cristata*	1		
	Cyanocorax dickeyi	1-h[2]		
	Aphelocoma ultramarina		1-h	
Hardwood and scrub........	*Calocitta formosa*	1-h		
	Aphelocoma coerulescens	½[3]	½	
	Cyanocorax yncas	1		
Pastures mixed with woodlands................	*Psilorhinus mexicanus*	1-h		
	Pica pica	1		
	Corvus coronoides	1		
Cultivated fields, and plains mixed with woodlands.....	*Corvus corone*	1		
	Corvus brachyrhynchos	½	½	
	Cyanopica cyana		½	½
Coniferous..................	*Gymnorhinus cyanocephala*			1
Desert				
Scrub......................	*Corvus cryptoleucus*	1		
	Corvus ruficollis	1		
Grassland..................	*Corvus capensis*	1		
Grassland				
Cultivated fields and pastures..................	*Corvus monedula*			1
	Corvus frugilegus			1
Savanna....................	*Pica nuttalli*		1	
	Corvus mellori		1	
Seashore.....................	*Corvus caurinus*			1
	Corvus ossifragus			1
Cliffs				
On seashore and alpine......	*Pyrrhocorax*			2
Total		17, ½, ½	3, ½, ½, ½	7, ½

[1] The numbers indicate species.
[2] Helpers at the nest indicated by h.
[3] A fractional entry indicates different dispersion types in parts of species range.

loosely colonial, colonial, and communal. Among corvids, as far as is known, only the first three types occur, of which solitary nesting is most common (table 11). Corvids occurring in forests and deserts (of which there are nine species) nest solitarily, while six species living along seashores, in high rugged mountains, and on cultivated fields nest colonially. Two loosely colonial species inhabit savannas. The remaining thirteen species occur in woodland, or mixtures of woodland with scrub, pastures, or cultivated fields. Of these species eight nest solitarily, one is loosely colonial, one is colonial, and three are solitary or loosely colonial, and loosely colonial or colonial in different parts of their range. Interestingly, no species of corvid shows all three types of nesting dispersion; this indicates conformity to a basic habitat. One would expect the wide-ranging Raven, not classified in table 11, to show all three types, but apparently it does not. To further summarize table 11, solitary nesting occurs in forests, deserts, and habitats associated with woodlands that are varied in composition. In these habitats the food is assumed to be more or less evenly dispersed, presumably richest in mixed woodlands and least abundant in deserts. Colonial nesting is found along seashores, on cultivated fields, and in those species that are specialized feeders, such as the Piñon Jay (*Gymnorhinus cyanocephala*). These species then breed where food is locally abundant. The loosely colonial forms breed in intermediate areas, where food is locally abundant but sparsely distributed elsewhere, as is the case for the Yellow-billed Magpie.

The fact that corvids are mated for life and do not normally breed until their second year, so that non-breeding birds make up part of the population, provides for the development of varied exploitation systems (fig. 19). Three aspects of figure 19 merit special discussion—the relationship among yearlings and adults, the territory (home range) and its exclusiveness, and the food supply and its distribution. In the Scrub Jay, yearlings are excluded from the territory (3 ha) and home range (3 ha) at all times, and feed in areas unoccupied by adults. These are away from edge situations, where adults hold territories, and are in general less favorable. In the Yellow-billed Magpie, yearlings are excluded from the territory (1 ha) but they can exploit the breeding home range (40 ha) although they seldom do. Yearling Rooks are excluded from the territory (confined to nest and its surroundings). They do, however, exploit the breeding home range (1,200 ha, calculated from Pinowski, 1959). Within this series there is a decrease in territory size, as more birds pack into a small area, and in the exclusiveness of the breeding home range, as the latter expands. As the area becomes larger, it becomes more difficult to defend.

The Mexican Jay (*Aphelocoma ultramarina*) has a loosely colonial nesting dispersion, with nests from 2 m to as much as 250 m apart (Brown, 1963a). The yearlings live within the home range of the adults and together with them form a flock whose membership changes but little and which collectively defends the home range. In these territorial groups, the yearling birds function as helpers (Hardy, 1961; Brown, 1963a). The Tufted Jay has the same system, with the addition that, so far as known, only one adult pair breeds, while other adults and yearlings assist in this effort (Crossin, 1967). The home range of the Mexican Jay (10 ha, calculated from Brown, 1963a, but probably smaller than average)

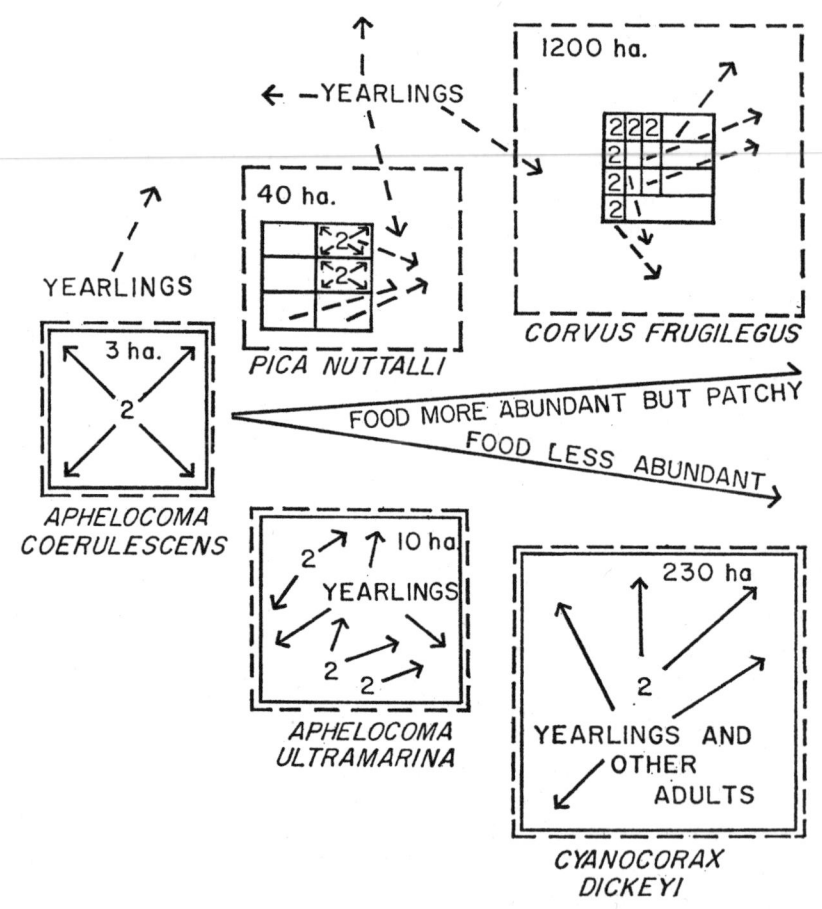

Fig. 19. Types of exploitation systems among corvids. Solid squares (territory boundaries), broken squares (home range), solid arrow (territorial defence and range of food procurement), dashed arrow (food procurement outside territory). Numbers inside squares (breeding pairs).

and that of the Tufted Jay (230 ha, calculated from Crossin, 1967) are rather stable and are exclusive, although few signs of defense have been seen. Socially these two species show a high degree of cooperation. An additional system, in which several adults lay eggs in one nest, might be expected, theoretically, to occur among corvids but none is known.

The Steller Jay maintains a year-round "territory," which is to be seen as a "series of concentric zones of diminishing dominance rank from the center of its nesting area outward" (Brown, 1963b). Within the population such zones overlap those of neighboring pairs. The central area of any individual is not defended except in the breeding season, but even then defense is not consistent (Brown, 1963b). The exploitation system of the Steller Jay is not included in figure 19 because the available literature (Bent, 1946; Brown, 1963b) does not provide a clear picture of absolute size of territory or home range. Furthermore, there is no information on what proportion of the food is derived from the core area of each territory and what proportion from the area beyond it. In other words, while Brown (1963b) describes dominance in relation to territory, he does not tell us if the most dominant bird has the largest home range.

It would appear from Brown's report that Steller Jays in his study area were rather packed together for so large a bird (Brown, 1963b, fig. 1). To what extent this results from an enriched environment (food from the picnic area) is difficult to say, but I think that it may be the major factor in the strong expression of hierarchy in the territorial system he studied. It would be profitable to study the Steller Jay in an area uninfluenced by man. I would not be surprised if such a study showed the hierarchical pattern to be weak or absent, and revealed conformity to the system found in other forest-dependent corvids, such as the Clark's Nutcracker (Mewaldt, 1956) and the Gray Jay (*Perisoreus canadensis*) (Rutter, 1969).

The exclusion or inclusion of yearlings from the home range or territory and the presence or absence of cooperation are related to food supply, as suggested in figure 19. As noted, the Scrub Jay has a broad niche and exploits a varied habitat of woodland, scrub, and grassland. Its food supply is sparse and both distributed and exploited randomly. In the Yellow-billed Magpie, more than half of the nestling food comes from patchy, abundant, but unpredictable and shifting food supplies at considerable distances from the nest. Because of the area and flight distances in foraging, the exclusive territory is less important as a food source than it is for the Scrub Jay, and it is, in fact, just a small fraction of the foraging area or home range. The Rook feeds on locally abundant foods that are more predictable, and usually nests near to them. Defense of such a food supply is unnecessary and impractical. This results in considerable overlap of the feeding areas of neighboring colonies (Roebuck, 1933). The questions remain why the Yellow-billed Magpie does not nest closer to its food supply, and why it is not colonial. The answer to the first question is found in the unpredictable distribution and abundance of those foods on which it relies. Those nests that are located in an average position in relation to these shifting centers of food abundance have proved to be successful in the past and serve as a focal point for young birds breeding for the first time. The answer to the second question involves the same unpredictable food supply. The maintenance of an exclusive territory, although small in relation to the total food requirement, nevertheless serves as some insurance when the more important food supply fails. I think that these two points are a better explanation for the evolution of nesting dispersion in loosely colonial systems, at least in the Yellow-billed Magpie, than Lack's (1968) suggestion that this dispersion results from predator avoidance.

In the evolution of the exploitation system of the Mexican Jay, two significant ecological changes have occurred: abandonment of the pair-held territory, and the incorporation of yearlings and unpaired adults into the nesting effort. Along with these changes, one finds adjustments in behavior and morphology (Hardy, 1961; Brown, 1963a, 1971). As both old and young defend the home range they must have a vested interest in what it has to offer, presumably food.

The habitat requirements of the Mexican Jay are narrower, and the habitat is more patchy, than those of the Scrub Jay (Pitelka, 1951; Hardy, 1961). Oaks are required (Marshall, 1957). We know regrettably little about the food habits of the Mexican Jay, but data in Bent (1946) and Westcott (1969) indicate acorns to be very important. Although the Scrub Jay feeds acorns to its nestlings (Verbeek, 1970), they form a small part of the diet compared with invertebrates. The same probably holds true for the Mexican Jay. The supply of acorns is greatest in fall, and although many are buried, very few are left next spring. Brown (1963a) did not see Mexican Jays with acorns in February and April. Additionally, acorn abundance fluctuates unpredictably from year to year. Whereas yearling Scrub Jays, because of the wider habitat range of the species, successfully exist in marginal habitats, the Mexican Jay presumably makes limited use of marginal habitats, because it probably does not favor the survival of yearlings.

Invertebrate food is presumed to be scarce during the breeding season, in part because of the narrow habitat range, and in part because the ground vegetation does not begin to grow until the rainy season in July (Marshall, 1957), which is well past the breeding season. Feeding is thus restricted largely to the canopy of trees and shrubs. If food were abundant, then this, along with the aid of assistants in the nesting cycle (Gross, 1949; others), would be expected to lead to a larger clutch, and a shorter nestling period. In neither respect, however, does the Mexican Jay differ from other species of jay, such as the Steller Jay or Scrub Jay.

I assume that at one time the Mexican Jay, like the Scrub Jay, maintained large pair-held, year-round territories. Perhaps with increasing aridity, food became more scarce and territories so large that their defense was no longer practical. This led to more social habits and to the participation of yearlings in a flock. Collectively, the birds in the flock were better able to locate and exploit food patches. Once the yearlings became an integral part of adult society the way was opened to their assistance in the breeding effort. Although the presence of the yearlings is an additional drain on the scarce food supply, this disadvantage is presumed to be outweighed by the increased chance of finding patches of food and by more effective defense of the territory. Also, with additional helpers at the nest, the energy expended in finding this scarce food is spread more thinly over several birds. This is shown clearly by Brown (1971), who found that the feeding rate at two nests, with 13 and 11 birds feeding the nestlings, was 5.2 and 3.5 feedings per hour. This is less than the feeding rate of the Yellow-billed Magpie (table 7) in which case only two birds fed the young. Those pairs that did not allow helpers produced fewer offspring than those that did allow them. The evolution of this helper system is supported by the fact that, as in other corvids, young birds do not normally breed until two years old. There are no data to the contrary. In return for its assistance a yearling benefits by gaining experience and by being able to feed in more productive areas; and by participating in a flock, it helps to insure its own existence.

These suggestions are in disagreement with Brown's (1971) altruistic explanation. Altruism, according to Brown, involves the sacrificing of an individual's own fitness to enhance the fitness of other individuals. My objection is to the use of the world "altruism," because it implies that the assistance given by helpers to other members of the flock is of no benefit to themselves. Membership in the flock is beneficial to all that belong to it. In other words, the helpers are helping to help themselves! I further wonder if a bird can be considered to sacrifice its own fitness when even the most active yearling fed the nestlings in two nests only 20 times in 113.5 hours, i.e., one feeding for each 5.7 hours. Lastly, the evolution of an altruistic trait theoretically can only develop where individuals in a group are genetically closely related (Hamilton, 1963). Unfortunately, we know little about the Mexican Jay outside of the breeding season, and we do not know whether the young of one year stay with the flock to help raise the young of the next year, or whether there is a dispersal and mixing of young at some phase of the annual cycle.

The Tufted Jay has a system similar to that of the Mexican Jay, with the addition that only two adults in a flock breed, while other adults and yearlings assist them. As in the Mexican Jay, the habitat is narrow, restricted in Crossin's (1967) study area to canyon bottoms where oaks predominated. The birds are primarily vegetarians and feed mostly in trees. This could indicate a niche and a habitat preference that are yet narrower than those of the Mexican Jay. I suggest that the same arguments used regarding the Mexican Jay may apply to the Tufted Jay. This system is not wasteful, as suggested by Crossin (1967). On the contrary, this exploitation system appears to be the logical consequence of narrow niche and restricted habitat; other things being equal, it would be more wasteful if all adults bred.

SUMMARY

The distribution, abundance, and availability of food vary with seasonal shifts in weather and daylength. This paper deals with the behavioral adaptations of the Yellow-billed Magpie to these changing aspects of food and time.

The study was conducted on the Hastings Reservation, Monterey County, California, and covers all months of the year from 15 June 1967 until 31 May 1971. Magpies were color-banded for individual recognition. I sampled insects in the field from March 1969 until May 1971. In addition, nestling food habits were obtained from 1968 to 1970. Climatic data are provided.

Magpies mate for life and appear to do so as early as the fall of the year in which they are born. Normally they breed when two years old. Adults maintain year-round territories in a loose colony. Territories are largest in area (ca. 1 ha) and most exclusive during the breeding season, and smallest in area in the summer months when the birds are frequently absent because they wander. Territories are re-established in the fall when birds breeding for the first time enter the colony. Behavior associated with maintenance of the pair bond and with copulation is described. Courtship begging serves to stimulate the male to feed the female during incubation.

Each year the birds build a new nest, which lasts, on the average, for 6 years. The mean distance between nests located in territories connected by a continuous canopy was 31 m. Three times two pairs nested in the same tree at distances of 7 and 12 m. Average height of 29 nests was 16.9 m. Both sexes build the nest, construction taking about 10 weeks.

After completion of the nest comes a rest period of about 10 days, during which the birds feed intensively. This is followed by egg laying. Incubation begins before completion of the clutch. Nest attentiveness is 92.3 percent. The average inattentive period is 4.1 minutes. Early in incubation the male obtains food primarily from the territory, but progressively more food is obtained away from it. At hatching almost all food comes from areas as far as 1 km from the nest. While the female continues to obtain food from these distant sources, the male slowly reverts to feeding on the territory. Males molt earlier than females. The beginning of molt about midway through the nestling period is suggested as the reason that the male reverts to feeding on the territory. Early nests fledge more young than later ones. Distant food supplies are found by individual exploration and then mutually exploited. This habit is considered important in the evolution of the semi-colonial nesting dispersion.

During the breeding season yearlings continue to flock. Once the young are independent, adults and juveniles join the yearlings, and magpies of several colonies flock together. The largest flocks occur in the summer months. Six roosting assemblages are described on the basis of seasonal occupancy and participation of the various age classes.

The discussion compares the exploitation systems of the Yellow-billed Magpie and the Scrub Jay. Timing of the breeding season to take advantage of peak food supply is found in both species. Courtship feeding prior to egg laying in the Scrub Jay, and a clutch which, in proportion to body weight, weighs less in the jay than in the magpie, are suggested as reasons that the jay lays its eggs earlier than the magpie. Both species molt during the summer at a time of reduced food abundance. Differences in the timing of molt and the total period of molt in adults and juveniles are related to the period of fledgling dependence and to the width of the niche and feeding repertoire. Flocking is related to food supply and habitat.

A survey of corvid nesting dispersion types shows that most corvids nest solitarily in habitats classified as forests, woodlands of varying structure and composition, and deserts. Nesting dispersion is related to dispersion of food. In conclusion, five corvid exploitation systems are compared, with particular attention to the relationship among yearlings and adults, territory and its exclusiveness, and the food supply and its distribution.

ACKNOWLEDGMENTS

I am indebted to Frank A. Pitelka for his continued support and stimulation throughout this study. I thank him, Herbert G. Baker, John Davis, and Oliver P. Pearson for discussion and important improvements of the manuscript. John Davis, James Griffin, James Bell, and the other residents at the Hastings Reservation were most cooperative throughout and created a helpful atmosphere that made our stay a pleasure. Gene M. Christman gave advice concerning the many diagrams.

Financial assistance from a Chapman Grant from the American Museum of Natural History is gratefully acknowledged. For the loan and use of specimens I thank Dean Amadon, Emmet R. Blake, and Robert T. Orr.

My wife, Linda, collected the data on primary productivity of the grassland. She was most helpful in discussion, and in editing and typing of the manuscript.

APPENDIX
A WHO'S WHO OF MARKED BREEDING BIRDS IN THE HASTINGS COLONY, 1967–71

Sex	Colors	Age	Date caught	History
♂	Blue	Adult	23 June 1967	Mated to unbanded female until November 1968. Remated with RW until September 1969. Remated with RG and still mated at end of study.
♀	Blue Blue	Adult	1 July 1967	Mated to RY and paired to him until end of study.
♂	White Green	Adult	14 May 1968	Mated to a female with a crooked leg until fall of 1967. Remated in October and retained mate until 2 May 1970 when she was killed by a predator. Remated 21 June or earlier and retained mate until end of study.
♀	Red Green	Yearling	25 Aug 1968	Mated to YY at time of capture. Remated with B in fall of 1969.
♂	Yellow Yellow	Adult	30 Aug 1968	Mated to RG and disappeared May 1969 while young were still in nest.
♂	Red Yellow	Adult	24 Sept 1968	Mated to BB until end of study.
♀	Red White	Adult	25 April 1969	Mated to B in January 1968 and paired with him until September 1969 when she disappeared.
♂	Blue Red	Immature	27 Aug 1969	Mated to another unbanded immature and still paired with her at end of study.
♀	Yellow Yellow	Adult	21 Feb 1970	Mated to unbanded male when they arrived in the colony from elsewhere in May 1969. Still mated at end of study.

LITERATURE CITED

BÄHRMANN, U.
- 1952. Ein Beitrag zur Biologie der Elster (*Pica pica pica* L.) Bonn. Zool. Beitr. 3:289–304.
- 1956. Welchen Einfluss hatte der Winter 1955/56 auf den Brutzyklus der Elster? Falke 3:195–198.
- 1968. Die Elster (*Pica pica*). Die Neue Brehm-Bücherei 393. A. Ziemsen Verlag.

BENT, A. C.
- 1946. Life histories of North American jays, crows, and magpies. U. S. Nat. Mus. Bull. 191.

BOCK, W. J.
- 1962. Feather tracts of the Corvidae—a correction. Ibis 104:257–259.

BORGVALL, T.
- 1952. En overnattningsplats for kajor och krakor i Goteborg. Vår Fågelvärld 11:11–15.

BROWN, J. L.
- 1963a. Social organization and behavior of the Mexican Jay. Condor 65:126–153.
- 1963b. Aggressiveness, dominance, and social organization in the Steller Jay. Condor 65:460–484.
- 1971. Cooperative breeding and altruistic behaviour in the Mexican Jay, *Aphelocoma ultramarina*. Anim. Behav. 18:366–378.

BROWN, R. H.
- 1924. Field-notes on the magpies, as observed in Cumberland. Brit. Birds 18:122–128.

BROWN, R. L.
- 1957. The population ecology of the magpie in western Montana, Unpublished M.S. thesis, Montana State Univ., Missoula, Montana.

BURCKHARDT, D.
- 1954. Beitrag zur embryonalen Pterylose einiger Nesthocker. Revue Suisse de Zoologie 61:551–633.

CARNIE, K.
- 1954. Food habits of nesting Golden Eagles in the coast ranges of California. Condor 56:1–12.

CARRICK, R.
- 1963. Ecological significance of territory in the Australian Magpie, *Gymnorhina tibicen*. Proc. XIII Intern. Ornithol. Congr.: 740–753.

COOMBS, C. J. F.
- 1960. Observations on the Rook *Corvus frugilegus* in southwest Cornwall. Ibis 102:394–419.

COWARD, T. A.
- 1920. Birds of the British Islands and their eggs. 1st series. F. Warne and Co. Ltd. London and New York.

CROOK, J. H.
- 1965. The adaptive significance of avian social organizations. Symp. Zool. Soc. London 14:181–218.

CROSSIN, R. S.
- 1967. The breeding biology of the Tufted Jay. Proc. Western Found. Vert. Zool. 1:265–299.

DARWIN, C.
- 1874. The descent of man and selection in relation to sex. John Murray, London.

DWIGHT, J., JR.
- 1900. The sequence of plumages and moults of the passerine birds of New York, Annals N. Y. Acad. Sci. 13:73–360.

EISENBERG, J. F.
- 1966. The social organizations of mammals. Handbuch der Zoologie. Walter de Gruyter, Berlin. 8:1–92.

ERPINO, M. J.
- 1968a. Age determination in the Black-billed Magpie. Condor 70:91–92.
- 1968b. Nest-related activities of Black-billed Magpies. Condor 70:154–165.
- 1969. Seasonal cycle of reproductive physiology in the Black-billed Magpie. Condor 71:267–279.

FUCHS, W.
   1957. Frühzeitige Paarbildung bei Elstern. Orn. Beob. 54:136.
GOODWIN, D.
   1952. Notes and display of the magpie. Brit. Birds 45:112–122.
GROSS, A. O.
   1949. Nesting of the Mexican Jay in the Santa Rita Mountains, Arizona. Condor 51:241–249.
GWINNER, E.
   1964. Untersuchungen über das Ausdrucks- und Sozialverhalten des Kolkraben (*Corvus corax corax* L.). Z. Tierpsychol. 21:657–748.
   1966. Über Bau und Funktion einer Nickhautstruktur der Elster (*Pica pica*). J. Orn. 107:323–325.
HAARTMAN, L., VON
   1969. Nest-site and evolution of polygamy in European passerine birds. Ornis Fennica 46:1–12.
HAASE, B. L.
   1963. The winter flocking behavior of the Common Crow (*Corvus brachyrhynchos* Brehm). Ohio J. Sci. 63:145–151.
HAMILTON, W. D.
   1963. The evolution of altruistic behavior. Am. Nat. 97:354–356.
HANSEN, L.
   1950. An investigation of the occurrence, nest building, etc. of the magpie, *Pica pica* (L.). Dansk Orn. Foren. Tidsskr. 44:150–161.
HARDY, J. W.
   1961. Studies in behavior and phylogeny of certain new world jays (Garrulineae). Univ. Kansas Sci. Bull. 42:13–149.
HEADY, H. F.
   1958. Vegetational changes in the California annual type. Ecology 39:402–416.
HINDE, R. A.
   1956. The biological significance of the territories of birds. Ibis 98:340–369.
HOLMES, R. T.
   1966. Breeding ecology and annual cycle adaptations of the Red-backed Sandpiper (*Calidris alpina*) in northern Alaska. Condor 68:3–46.
HOLYOAK, D.
   1967. Breeding biology of the Corvidae. Bird Study 14:153–168.
HORN, H. S.
   1968. The adaptive significance of colonial nesting in the Brewer's Blackbird (*Euphagus cyanocephalus*). Ecology 49:682–694.
HOSONO, T.
   1966. A study of the life history of the Blue Magpie (I) 1. Breeding biology. Misc. Repts. Yamashina Inst. Orn. Zool. 4:327–347.
   1967. A study of the life history of the Blue Magpie. 2. Roosting behavior (1). Misc. Repts. Yamashina Inst. Orn. Zool. 5:34–47.
HUBER, J.
   1944. Aus dem Leben der Elster im Sempacherseegebiet. Orn. Beob. 41:1–7.
JONES, R. E.
   1960. Activities of the Magpie during the breeding period in southern Idaho. Northwest Sci. 34:18–24.
KILLPACK, M. L.
   1951. Short-eared Owl eaten by Horned Owl. Condor 53:262.
KRAMER, G.
   1932. Beobachtungen und Fragen zur Biologie des Kolkraben. J. Orn. 80:329–342.
LABITTE, A.
   1953. Quelques notes sur la biologie et la reproduction de la pie bavarde. Oiseau 23:247–260.

LACK, D.
1954. The natural regulation of animal numbers. Clarendon Press, Oxford.
1966. Population studies of birds. Clarendon Press, Oxford.
1968. Ecological adaptations for breeding in birds. Methuen, London.

LAMM, D. W.
1958. A nesting study of the Pied Crow at Accra, Ghana. Ostrich 29:59–70.

LINSDALE, J. M.
1937. The natural history of magpies. Pac. Coast Avif. No. 25.
1946. Yellow-billed Magpie, *in:* Life histories of North American jays, crows, and titmice, by A. C. Bent. U. S. Nat. Mus. Bull. 191.

LOFTS, B., and R. K. MURTON
1968. Photoperiodic and physiological adaptations regulating avian breeding cycles and their ecological significance. J. Zool. Lon. 155:327–394.

LORENZ, K.
1931. Beiträge zur Ethologie sozialer Corviden. J. Orn. 79:67–120.
1940. Die Paarbildung beim Kolkraben. Z. Tierpsychol. 3:287–292.

LOWE, P. R.
1938. Some anatomical and other notes on the systematic position of the genus *Picathartes*, together with some remarks on the families Sturnidae and Eulebetidae. Ibis 80:254–269.

MARSHALL, J. F., JR.
1957. Birds of the pine-oak woodland in southern Arizona and adjacent Mexico. Pac. Coast Avif. No. 32.

MAYAUD, N.
1933. Notes et remarques sur quelques Corvides. I. Le Crave *Pyrrhocorax pyrrhocorax* (L.). Alauda 2:195–216.

McGAHAN, J.
1968. Ecology of the Golden Eagle. Auk 85:1–12.

MEWALDT, L. R.
1956. Nesting behavior of the Clark Nutcracker. Condor 58:3–23.
1958. Pterylography and natural and experimentally induced molt in Clark's Nutcracker. Condor 60:165–187.

NIETHAMMER, G.
1937. Handbuch der Deutschen Vogelkunde. Band 1. Akad. Verlagsgesellschaft, Leipzig.

NIETHAMMER, G., and E. MERZINGER
1943. Über Beteiligung des Brutgeschaftes nach Alter und Geschlecht. Beitr. Fortpl. Biol. Vögel 19:21–22.

O'HALLORAN, P. L.
1961. Dynamics of a reduced magpie population. Unpublished M.S. thesis, Montana State Univ., Missoula, Montana.

ORIANS, G. H.
1961. The ecology of blackbird (*Agelaius*) social systems. Ecol. Monogr. 31:285–312.
1969. On the evolution of mating systems in birds and mammals. Am. Naturalist 103:589–603.

PEARSON, O. P.
1954. The daily energy requirements of a wild Anna Hummingbird. Condor 56:317–322.

PERRINS, C. M.
1970. The timing of birds' breeding seasons. Ibis 102:242–255.

PINOWSKI, J.
1959. Factors influencing the number of feeding rooks (*Corvus frugilegus frugilegus* L.) in various field environments. Ekol. Polska, Seria A. 16:1–48.

PITELKA, F. A.
1945. Pterylography, molt, and age determination of American jays of the genus *Aphelocoma*. Condor 47:229–261.
1951. Speciation and ecologic distribution in American jays of the genus *Aphelocoma*. Univ. Calif. Publ. Zool. 50:195–464.

1958. Timing of molt in the Steller Jays of the Queen Charlotte Islands, British Columbia. Condor 60:38–49.

1959. Numbers, breeding schedule, and territoriality in Pectoral Sandpipers of Northern Alaska. Condor 61:233–264.

PITELKA, F. A., P. Q. TOMICH, and G. W. TREICHEL
1955. Ecological relations of jaegers and owls as lemming predators near Barrow, Alaska. Ecol. Monogr. 25:85–117.

ROEBUCK, A.
1933. A survey of the rooks in the Midlands. Brit. Birds 27:4–23.

ROOT, R. B.
1967. The niche exploitation pattern of the Blue-gray Gnatcatcher. Ecol. Monogr. 37:317–350.

ROWLEY, I.
1967. Sympatry in Australian Ravens. Proc. Ecol. Soc. Aust. 2:107–115.

RUTTER, R. J.
1969. A contribution to the biology of the Gray Jay (*Perisoreus canadensis*). Can. Field-Nat. 83:300–316.

RYDER, J. P.
1970. A possible factor in the evolution of clutch size in Ross' Goose. Wilson Bull. 82:5–13.

SCHOENER, T. W.
1968. Sizes of feeding territories among birds. Ecol. 49:123–141.

SELOUS, E.
1927. Realities of bird life. Constable and Co. Ltd. London.

SHANNON, G. R.
1958. Magpie's rapid replacement of dead mate. Brit. Birds 51:401–402.

SKEAD, C. J.
1952. A study of the Black Crow *Corvus capensis*. Ibis 94:434–451.

SKUTCH, A. F.
1960. Life histories of Central American birds. Part 2. Families Vireonidae through Tyrannidae. Pac. Coast Avif. No. 34.

STEINFATT, O.
1943. Einige Beobachtungen über die Elster. Beitr. Fortpl. Biol. Vögel 19:68–71.

STEWART, W.
1910. Ceremonial gatherings of the magpies. Brit. Birds 4:188.

TINBERGEN, N.
1967. Adaptive features of the Black-headed Gull *Larus ridibundus* L. Proc. Int. Orn. Congr. 14:43–59.

TINKLE, D. W., H. M. WILBUR, and S. G. TILLEY
1970. Evolutionary strategies in lizard reproduction. Evolution 24:55–74.

TOMPA, F. S.
1964. Factors determining the numbers of Song Sparrows *Melospiza melodia* (Wilson) on Mandarte Isl. B. C., Canada. Acta Zool. Fennica 109:1–73.

VERBEEK, N. A. M.
1964. A time and energy budget study of the Brewer Blackbird. Condor 66:70–74.
1970. Feeding ecology of two coexisting corvids, *in* N. A. M. Verbeek, The exploitation system of the Yellow-billed Magpie. Unpublished Ph.D. dissertation, University of California, Berkeley.
1972. Daily and annual time budget of the Yellow-billed Magpie. Auk 89:567–582.

VERNER, J., and M. F. WILSON
1966. The influence of habitats on mating systems of North American passerine birds. Ecology 47:143–147.

WESTCOTT, P. W.
1969. Relationships among three species of jays wintering in southeastern Arizona. Condor 71:353–359.

WHITE, K. L.
1966a. Structure and composition of foothill woodland in central coastal California. Ecology 47:229–237.
1966b. Old-field succession on Hastings Reservation, California. Ecology 47:865–868.

WITHERBY, H. F., F. C. JOURDAIN, N. F. TICEHURST, and B. W. TUCKER
1940. The handbook of British birds. Vol. I. Witherby, London.

WITTENBERG, J.
1968. Freilanduntersuchungen zu Brutbiologie und Verhalten der Rabenkrahe (*Corvus c. corone*). Zool. Jb. Syst. 95:16–146.

WYNNE-EDWARDS, V. C.
1962. Animal dispersion in relation to social behaviour. Hafner Publishing Co., New York.